The African-American Heritage Cookbook

The African-American Heritage Cookbook

Traditional Recipes and Fond Remembrances From Alabama's Renowned Tuskegee Institute

Carolyn Quick Tillery

A Birch Lane Press Book
Published by Carol Publishing Group

Material quoted herein from *Benjamin O. Davis Jr., American: An Autobiography*, foreword by L. Douglas Wilder (Washington, D.C.: Smithsonian Institution Press), pp. 129–31, by permission of the publisher. Copyright 1991.

A Birch Lane Press Book
Published by Carol Publishing Group

Birch Lane Press is a registered trademark of Carol Communications, Inc.

Editorial, sales and distribution, rights and permissions inquiries should be addressed to Carol Publishing Group, 120 Enterprise Avenue, Secaucus, N.J. 07094

In Canada: Canadian Manda Group, One Atlantic Avenue, Suite 105, Toronto, Ontario M6K 3E7

Carol Publishing Group books may be purchased in bulk at special discounts for sales promotion, fund-raising, or educational purposes. Special editions can be created to specifications. For details, contact Special Sales Department, 120 Enterprise Avenue, Secaucus, N.J. 07094.

Manufactured in the United States of America

ISBN 1-55972-325-4 (hardcover)

In Remembrance of Dr. Luther H. Foster,

fourth president of Tuskegee Institute

In 1941, Dr. Foster came to Tuskegee, where for twelve years he served as business manager. On June 1, 1953, he assumed the presidency. As a manager, educator, and team builder, he provided visionary leadership to Tuskegee through the challenging times of World War II, fiscal austerity, and national and student unrest. He instituted many revolutionary changes that strengthened Tuskegee's reputation for educational accomplishment.

In his graduation message to the class of 1979 he stated, "[You] will carry with you credentials from a strong and viable institution, whose programs and services are known and respected throughout this country and in overseas places as well. We are confident that you will help extend Tuskegee's reputation and render service in the true spirit of this place. You have been associated with an Institution that has a deep commitment to the uplift of disadvantaged people—an important part of the Tuskegee Mission—and this has been a splendid characteristic of the thousands of alumni who serve their communities so well. We know that you, too, will carry on this example of Tuskegee's great heritage."

I am a proud member of the class of '79 in which Dr. Foster placed so much trust. However, but for Dr. Foster, I would not have graduated. During my first year, I socialized more than I studied. Placed on academic probation, I made a tearful telephone call to Dr. Foster at his home on a Sunday afternoon. Dr. Foster graciously accepted my call, told me not to cry, and promised to take care of it. He did. He gave me a second chance. I came back and made the honor roll. Years later, after serving as an Air Force officer, completing law school, a clerkship for a former state supreme court justice, and an assignment as an assistant district attorney, I called Dr. Foster to thank him for giving me a second chance to succeed and serve. He said, "No problem, just remember to pass it on." I said, "Thank you, sir, I will. . . . I promise."

CONTENTS

THE TUSKEGEE SONG

Tuskegee, thou pride of the swift growing South,
We pay thee our homage today,
For the worth of thy teaching, the joy of thy care;
And the good we have known 'neath thy sway.
Oh, long-striving mother of diligent Sons,
And of Daughters, whose strength is their pride,
We will love thee forever, and ever shall walk
Thro' the oncoming years at thy side.

Thy hand we have held up the difficult steeps.
When painful and slow was the pace,
And onward and upward we've labored with thee
For the glory of God and our race.
The fields smile to greet us, the forests are glad,
The ring of the anvil and hoe
Have a music as thrilling and sweet as a harp
Which thou taught us to hear and to know.

Oh, Mother Tuskegee, thou shinest today
As a gem in the fairest of lands;
Thou gavest the heav'n-blessed power to see
The worth of our minds and our hands.
We thank thee, we bless thee, we pray for thee years,
Imploring with grateful accord,
Full fruit for thy striving, time longer to strive,
Sweet love and true labor's reward.

PAUL LAURENCE DUNBAR,
Music by N. CLARK SMITH

INTRODUCTION

In 1881, Booker T. Washington, a Hampton Institute graduate, arrived in Tuskegee, Alabama. Washington had been invited there to teach and be principal at the legislatively approved school for blacks by Mr. Lewis Adams, a former slave, and Mr. George Campbell, a former slave owner. Upon his arrival the young teacher found a shanty beneath a chinaberry tree and another building with a roof so leaky that when it rained, a student had to hold an umbrella over his head while he continued to hear recitations. From this beginning, Washington created a black educational mecca of international repute. During his lifetime, the school's reputation grew, until by the time of his death, in 1915, it was the hallmark by which all others were measured.

Today Tuskegee, a humble, sleepy southern town, remains cloaked in a rich cultural heritage. As Timbuktu was to the ancients, so is Tuskegee to modern African Americans. Leaders of country and state—captains of industry—have sought out the wisdom of her leadership. Her children's names are forever engraved on the American roll call of greatness: Booker T. Washington's and his wives, Fanny, Olivia, and Margaret; George Washington Carver—a great scientist for whom public service was a sacred calling; Rosa Parks; Chief Anderson; Lt. Gen. Benjamin O. Davis Jr.; our own Black Eagles, the Tuskegee Airmen; "Chappie"; Lionel Richie; the Commodores; and Keenan Ivory Wayans. These beneficiaries of a legacy of excellence and tradition found their strength from those before them, often unsung heroes who arrived with little more than a hope for a better day. Men and women together, bending their backs low, lifting their hands high, and building a dream called Tuskegee.

The recipes and traditions of Tuskegee are a joyful celebration of hope triumphant. In those lean, hungry early years when Tuskegee was little more than a dream, food was central to survival. "Festivals" or "suppers," held to raise money, were an integral part of every celebration. Town people, both black and white, gave a cake, a chicken, bread, or pies that could be sold at the festival. Even the school's industries, which according to Booker T. Washington, "started in natural and logical order," began with farming because "we wanted something to eat."

Dr. George Washington Carver
(Library of Congress)

Concern with food and diet extended to the local community. Upon his arrival, Washington observed that the common diet of sharecroppers was fat pork, corn bread, and, on occasion, molasses. When they were without fat pork, sometimes their only food was the corn bread, served with black-eyed peas, cooked in plain water. Ironically, or perhaps purposefully, the landlords required cotton to be grown to the doorsteps of the cabin. As a result, sharecroppers could not raise their own food, but were required to buy everything from the expensive plantation commissary; consequently, they remained impoverished and dependent. Washington urged them to ask for a small plot of land on which to grow food and raise chickens. George Washington Carver showed them how to maximize production of the plots or to live off "nature's bounty" where no plot could be obtained. If the farmers could not come to him, Carver would load up his demonstration wagon (later known as the Jessup Wagon) and go to them. In later years, the farmers would gather at the institute once a year to share information, show off their accomplishments, and celebrate their successes. In addition to showing subsistence farmers methods of increasing their yield, Carver, an accomplished cook, shared recipes and preservation methods with their wives, and as a result, the women began to participate as well. A number of those

Carver recipes are included in this book. Additionally, some of his personal recollections are recorded, as well as those of Booker T. and his daughter Portia Washington.

The personal recollections of Washington and Carver, cited in this cookbook, give dimension and color to the meals and events they describe. The recipes that belonged to Dr. Carver are clearly identified by an asterisk. Those provided by other members of the Tuskegee community are also credited. However, the vast majority are traditional recipes, handed down from generation to generation—in the tradition of Tuskegee. In stories about food, such as the one described in Rackham Holt's biography, *George Washington Carver,* Carver, in colorful detail, describes the festive atmosphere of the fairs, as well as the food that was served.

The occasional observations and first-person anecdotes I have provided throughout the book are intended to be not a definitive history of Tuskegee, but an attempt to give a human dimension to Tuskegee's great men and women through their relationship to food and its preparation. The past can come alive in many ways. Sometimes we can learn more about a figure from history by preparing a meal that he or she may have loved than from studying books or poring over documents.

For example, a particularly poignant story is excerpted from Washington's famous autobiography, *Up From Slavery.* Washington, in sharing a memory from his childhood as a slave, recollects seeing his young mistresses and some lady visitors eating ginger cakes in the yard: "At that time those cakes seemed to me to be absolutely the most tempting and desirable things that I had ever seen; and I then and there resolved that, if I ever got free, the height of my ambition would be reached if I could get to the point where I could secure and eat ginger cakes in the way that I saw those ladies doing."

The recipe that follows the narrative is traditional to the period. While many recipes have been lost to us, these recollections permit us a glimpse into the private thoughts and lives of these national treasures, the only two African Americans inducted into the American Hall of Fame.

These recipes are traditional and some are high in fat and calories. If you wish, you can easily make low-fat substitutions (smoked turkey is an excellent replacement for ham when cooking vegetables) and reduce the amount of sugar and salt used. You will eventually pass on new traditions; however, the old ones will be safely recorded for "remembrance." The recipes and recollections in this book combine to evoke the smell, emotions, and, yes, even the taste of Tuskegee in a way that cannot be adequately captured in a simple narrative of its history.

ACKNOWLEDGMENTS

I wish to express appreciation to my parents; husband, J.R.; daughter, Ashley; and "Missy." Thanks to Kevin McDonough, my editor—and to the ever-vigilant copyeditors. Additionally, I would like to thank the members of the Ebony Quill Writing Group. . . . And of course, my Tuskegee family, who have responded graciously and with their full support. A very special thanks to Mrs. Vera C. Foster, widow of Dr. Luther H. Foster. When I wrote and asked for support for this project, Mrs. Foster responded—in the true spirit of this place we call Tuskegee. Her recipes and comments appear just as she wrote them.

Author's Note

I have quoted a great deal of manuscript material in this collection from historical sources, including works by and about George Washington Carver, Booker T. Washington, and other figures central to the history of the Tuskegee Institute and African-American heritage. The original recipes are indicated with an asterisk after the title; they are presented here just as Dr. Carver wrote them. In some cases modern cooks will be required to make adjustments in the preparation. Some of the source material is cited in full, but for the reader's convenience I have used a shortened citation form throughout for those that are quoted most frequently. These abbreviations appear below. The full citations appear at the back of the book.

Carver, *Nature's Garden*
Carver, *The Peanut*
Carver, *Sweet Potatoes*
Davis, Autobiography
Harlan, *Booker T. Washington*
Hill, *Booker T's Child*
Holt, *George Washington Carver*
Stewart, *Portia*
Booker T. Washington Papers
Washington, *Up From Slavery*

THE AFRICAN-AMERICAN
HERITAGE COOKBOOK

BEVERAGES

I have the good fortune to count many Tuskegee classmates and fellow alumni among my friends and neighbors. I love having them over along with my family. Our laughter and fun continue long after the last ladle of punch is poured and the final dessert eaten. Amidst the hugs and kisses of our goodbyes, I lose track of who is an alumnus and who is family. I suppose that for Tuskegee graduates, they are one and the same.

GRANDMAMA'S SPICE TEA PUNCH

In later years a number of notables came to or through Tuskegee, and Portia Washington met many of them, including Ralph Ellison, her former music student, Marian Anderson, and Duke Ellington and his band. At a party to honor W. E. B. Du Bois, Portia met and danced with him . . . but with W. C. Handy, she had tea! (While we cannot be certain of the type of tea Portia and W. C. shared, this recipe is one typical of the period and is still served by various sororities on campus.)

1	1-inch cinnamon stick	1	quart water
20	whole cloves	1½	cups sugar
20	whole allspice berries	1	quart pineapple juice
3	tablespoons loose black tea		Lemon slices or fresh mint
3	tablespoons orange tea		for garnish
3	tablespoons cinnamon tea		
	or three bags of each tea type		

Tie spices in a cheesecloth bag. Contain loose tea according to package directions. Bring water to a rolling boil and remove pot from burner. Place tea and spice bag in hot water, and allow to steep 10 minutes. Remove tea and spices from water, add sugar, and mix well. Allow mixture to cool, place in a large non-metallic serving container, add juice, and refrigerate. Garnish with lemon slices or sprigs of fresh mint.

2 quarts, about 24 punch cup servings

ICED TEA SPRITZER

1¼ cups water
¾   cup sugar
¾   cup freshly squeezed lemon juice
2½ cups orange juice

¼   cup brewed unsweetened iced tea
4   12-ounce cans lemon-lime soda
    Orange wedges and maraschino
        cherries, for garnish

In a medium saucepan, combine water and sugar and stir over medium heat until sugar is dissolved. Remove from heat and cool about 20 minutes. Add remaining ingredients except garnishes. Mix well and serve in individual glasses, over cracked ice. Garnish with an orange wedge and maraschino cherry.

24 servings

APRICOT ICED TEA

4   orange pekoe tea bags
1   sprig mint
⅓   cup sugar

4¼ cups water
3½ cups apricot nectar

Place tea bags, mint, and sugar in a heatproof pitcher. In a saucepan, bring water to a boil and pour over tea bags, sugar, and mint. Steep 5 minutes and remove bags. Cool tea, add apricot nectar, and chill, covered, until cold, about 1 hour. Serve tea over cracked ice.

4 servings

STRAWBERRY TEA

4 to 6   tea bags
1½   cups sugar
1½   quarts cold water

1½   cups fresh strawberries
¼   cup water

Place tea bags and sugar in a heatproof pitcher. In a saucepan, bring cold water to a boil and pour over tea bags and sugar. Steep 5 minutes and remove bags. In a covered blender container, blend strawberries with ¼ cup water until smooth. If desired, strain purée to remove seeds by pressing through a sieve with the back of a spoon. Stir berry mixture into brewed tea. Cool tea and chill, covered, until cold, about an hour. Serve tea over cracked ice.

4 servings

"Around 1901 or 1902 my father had William Sidney Pittman design a mantel for our home. My father [knew] that I might have been interested in Pittman. . . . I was playing a piece called 'Narcissus.' . . . I played. I smiled, and we had a drink of lemonade. That is how we met."

PORTIA M. WASHINGTON PITTMAN,
quoted in Hill, *Booker T's Child*

OLD-FASHIONED LEMONADE

On Sunday evenings Sidney would call on her at The Oaks. At curfew Booker would call down from the top of the stairs, "Portia! ten o'clock." Then they would kiss at the bottom of the porch stairs.

8	lemons, 1 sliced thin	3	cups hot water
1½	cups sugar	1	quart cold water

Cover half of the sliced lemon with sugar; reserve the remainder for later use as a garnish. Squeeze the 7 remaining lemons, straining seeds from juice. Add juice to sliced lemons in the bowl. Cover with 3 cups of hot water. Do not stir. Allow to cool at room temperature. Transfer to a serving container; add the cold water. Adjust flavor to personal taste. Chill, and serve in frosted glasses over ice. Garnish with reserved fresh lemon slices. (To frost glasses, set them on a tray in the freezer compartment until covered with frost. Then dip rims in sugar and fill with lemonade or return unfilled glasses to the freezer for sugar to firmly set.)

6 to 8 servings

RED LEMONADE

"[And] the barbecued oxen and hogs and sheep were washed down with gallons of . . . red lemonade."

HOLT,
George Washington Carver

	Juice of 7 lemons	1	cup water
1½	cups sugar		Fresh mint sprigs and/or
1	quart water		lemon slices, for garnish
1½	pints fresh raspberries or 16 ounces frozen, unsweetened raspberries, thawed		

Combine lemon juice, sugar, and 1 quart water. Purée berries, place in a bowl, and cover with the cup of water. Strain berries through a sieve by gently pressing them with the back of a spoon. Mix strained raspberry juice with lemonade and add additional sugar to taste. Garnish with fresh mint sprigs and/or lemon slices.

6 servings

CLOVE LEMONADE

3 cups water	4¼ cups sugar
Juice of 8 lemons	Sparkling water and ice
1½ to 2 teaspoons ground cloves	

Combine 3 cups water, lemon juice, cloves, and sugar in a small saucepan. Bring to a boil over medium heat. Boil until sugar dissolves. Reduce heat and simmer 5 to 7 minutes. Allow syrup to cool and place ⅓ cup syrup in a tall glass. Fill glass with sparkling water and ice.

6 servings

SUMMER FRUIT PUNCH

2   cups orange juice
8   ounces frozen pineapple
      concentrate
¼   cup freshly squeezed lemon
      juice
2   tablespoons freshly squeezed
      lime juice

1   cup sugar
8   slices canned pineapple,
      including juice
2   quarts 7-Up
      Crushed ice

Mix together first 5 ingredients and refrigerate for at least 2 hours. Just before serving, place mixture in a punch bowl and add remaining ingredients.

24 servings

MAY DAY STRAWBERRY PUNCH

1   cup sugar
1   cup water
½   cup pineapple juice

1   teaspoon lemon juice
4   cups sliced strawberries
2   liters lemon-lime soda

In a small saucepan, combine the sugar and water; heat almost to boiling, stirring to dissolve the sugar. Remove from heat; stir in the juices. Chill. In a blender, purée berries. Add to juice mixture; chill 30 minutes. Transfer to punch bowl; add soda. If desired, float additional strawberries on top.

24 servings

APPETIZERS

Appetizers are the heart of a good party, or the perfect start to a sumptuous meal. The offerings in this chapter reflect the rich and varied backgrounds of the thousands of students who have come to Tuskegee from all over the world.

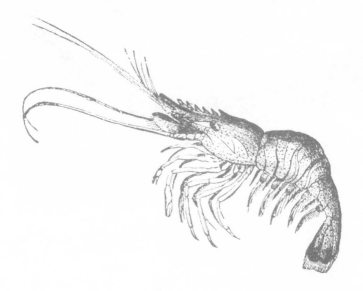

Spicy Papaya Salsa With Grilled Shrimp

SALSA

Prepare 1 day prior:

2	ripe, medium papayas, peeled and diced	1½	teaspoons grated fresh ginger
1	slightly firm avocado, peeled, pit removed, and diced	½	cup thinly sliced green onions
		2	tablespoons chopped cilantro
5	fresh, medium jalapeño peppers, seeded and chopped	1	garlic clove, minced
		¼	teaspoon chili powder
½	red bell pepper, diced	¼	teaspoon salt
		1½	tablespoons lime juice

Combine all of the above ingredients in a medium bowl and mix well. Cover and refrigerate overnight.

GRILLED SHRIMP

Prepare the next day:

	Mesquite chips for the grill	⅛	teaspoon ground cumin
15	wooden skewers	⅛	teaspoon chili powder
2½	pounds large shrimp	5	large garlic cloves, minced
½	cup freshly squeezed lemon juice	10	peppercorns
3	tablespoons olive oil	2	teaspoons minced chives

About 3 hours before grilling, soak mesquite chips in water or according to manufacturer's directions, and soak the wooden skewers in water to prevent burning. Shell and devein shrimp, leaving tails intact. In a large bowl, combine lemon juice, olive oil, spices, and remaining ingredients, including shrimp. Refrigerate 2 hours. Remove shrimp from refrigerator and allow to stand at room temperature 20 minutes prior to grilling. Prepare charcoal grill. When embers are glowing, spread about 2 cups of chips evenly over coals. Grill shrimp on skewers until pink and opaque, 3 to 5 minutes, being careful not to overcook. Serve with the salsa. This recipe goes well with Guacamole Dip and blue corn tortilla chips.

15 servings

RITA'S GRILLED SCALLOPS AND SHRIMP WITH BACON

My dear friend Rita Booker graciously shared this scrumptious recipe with me. Rita and her mother had the best pool parties and even slow-grilled turkey. . . . I'm still trying to get that recipe.

8 slices lean bacon	1 pound large shrimp, shelled
1 pound sea scallops	and deveined, tails left on

Blanch bacon in boiling water for about 3 minutes to remove some of the fat and to partially cook the bacon. Using either metal skewers or wooden ones that have been soaked in water, pierce one end of a bacon strip, then skewer a scallop. Bring bacon over top of scallop and skewer. Skewer a shrimp and bring bacon over top. Fill skewers, alternating bacon, scallops, and shrimp. Grill over hot charcoal or broil for about 8 minutes or until bacon is crisp.

6 servings

GARLIC SHRIMP

2	pounds large shrimp	¼	teaspoon ground cumin
1	cup olive oil	¼	teaspoon curry powder
7	garlic cloves, crushed		Seasoned salt to taste
1	teaspoon cayenne pepper, optional	¼	cup finely chopped green onions, for garnish

Shell and devein shrimp, leaving tails attached. Wash shrimp in cold water, dry, and place in a heatproof dish. Mix remaining ingredients except green onions, and pour over shrimp. Marinate in the refrigerator for 2 hours. Remove shrimp from dish, reserving the oil and seasonings.

Place dish, with reserved oils and seasonings, in a 400 degree F. oven until oil is hot. Be careful not to burn garlic. Quickly remove garlic, add shrimp, and return to the oven. Cook 3 to 5 minutes, until shrimp are pink and oil sizzles. Remove from oven, drain, stir in green onions, season with salt, and serve at once.

8 servings

GARLIC PRAWNS

	Olive oil	8 to 10	garlic cloves, crushed
18 to 21	green king prawns	⅓	cup chopped parsley
1	Scotch Bonnet or 3 small Anaheim peppers	1	teaspoon chopped cilantro

Half fill a large heatproof baking dish with oil; place in a 375 degree F. oven until oil is hot (or heat over a grill). Meanwhile, shell and clean prawns, leaving the tails attached. Halve chili peppers. When oil is sufficiently hot, add peppers, garlic, and prawns. Cook 3 to 5 minutes, turn prawns over, and cook an additional 3 to 5 minutes or until prawns are pink and oil is sizzling. Serve at once. Top with parsley and cilantro. Allow 3 prawns per serving.

6 to 7 servings

SHRIMP BOILED IN BEER

3 pounds large shrimp
36 ounces beer
8 garlic cloves, peeled and crushed
¼ cup Seafood Seasoning (page 66)
2 tablespoons salt
3 bay leaves
4 teaspoons Tabasco

1½ teaspoons celery seed
2 teaspoons cayenne pepper
Juice of 2 lemons
Butter or margarine, melted
    and seasoned to taste with
    additional Seafood
    Seasoning and Tabasco

Wash shrimp, but do not remove the shells. Combine the remaining ingredients except the lemon juice and butter and bring to a boil in a large pot. Add shrimp and bring to a second boil. Reduce heat to low and simmer, uncovered, until shrimp are pink and tender, approximately 2 to 5 minutes. Drain and serve with plenty of seasoned melted butter.

6 to 8 servings

TERIYAKI CHICKEN WINGS

1½ cups water
1 cup soy sauce
1½ cups pineapple juice
1¼ tablespoons Tabasco
¼ cup vegetable oil
1½ tablespoons ground ginger
3 tablespoons honey

3 tablespoons dark brown
    sugar
7 garlic cloves, crushed
30 to 40 chicken wings
1½ tablespoons cornstarch
¼ cup cold water
2 tablespoons honey

Combine water and next 8 ingredients. Split chicken at joints, and reserve tips for some other use. Pat dry, place in a large nonmetallic dish, and cover with marinade. Refrigerate overnight. Drain the chicken and reserve the marinade. Grill over hot coals or bake on a cookie sheet in a preheated 350 degree F. oven until done. Wings are done when you pierce the thickest part with a fork and juice runs clear. In a large skillet, bring reserved marinade to a boil; continue to boil for 5 minutes, stirring constantly; then reduce heat to low. Add cornstarch to cold water, and stir to form a paste. Slowly add paste to the simmering marinade, and stir as it thickens. Add 2 tablespoons honey and stir. When suitably thickened, return wings to skillet and coat. Set aside on a warm platter until ready to serve.

10 to 12 servings

"During WW II blacks were not permitted to serve in the U.S. Air Service, an elite officer flying corps. It was thought that black officers giving orders to white enlisted men would create social problems. Despite these opinions, Dr. Patterson invited Alfred 'Chief' Anderson to Tuskegee Institute in 1940 to start a flight training program. 'Chief' was the first black to receive a commercial pilot license in 1929 and the father of black aviation. First Lady Eleanor Roosevelt, in a public show of support and confidence, came to Tuskegee to be flown by flight trainer Chief Anderson. Despite her recommendations to the President, the strong opposition and public debate regarding the "fitness" of blacks to serve continued. However, in late spring of '41, B. O. Davis, Jr., received orders to Tuskegee. Subsequently, on July 10, 1941, the War Department announced that 'the first class of ten colored aviation cadets would begin training at Tuskegee Air Force Base.' Once trained, the cadets would serve with the newly activated all-black 99th Pursuit Squadron. Tuskegee was delighted and Dr. Patterson, the school's third president, secured money from the Rosenwald fund to purchase land for what would later be known as Moton Field. A school dormitory housed the trainees. 'For the next seven months I immersed myself in the miracle of flight.' 'In December we got the news . . . it was a Sunday afternoon . . . I was at Tuskegee Institute having a quiet dinner in a restaurant . . . "when it was learned" . . . the Japanese had bombed Pearl Harbor.' "

DAVIS,
Autobiography

Alfred "Chief" Anderson, piloting Eleanor Roosevelt in the *Booker T. Washington*
(*Tuskegee University Archives*)

"However, it was not until April 15, 1943, that they were deployed. Under the com-
mand of General B. O. Davis, Jr., the 99th Pursuit Squadron and the 332d Fighter
Group served with distinction. Over the course of the war . . . 450 black fighter pilots
. . . fought in the aerial war over North Africa, Sicily and Europe, flying P-40, P-39,
P-47 and P-51 type aircraft. Four squadrons, the 99th, the 100th, the 301st and the
302nd were the designated 332nd Fighter Group. These valiant men flew 15,553 sor-

ties and completed 1,578 bomber-escort missions over Europe with the 12th Tactical U.S. Army Air Force. They destroyed 409 enemy aircraft . . . theirs was the only squadron to sink a destroyer with gunfire. These brave men were called the 'Schwartze Vogelmenschen' (Black Birdmen) by the Germans . . . who both respected and feared them. White bomber crews are reported to have reverently referred to them as the Black Red Tail Angels because . . . of their reputation for not losing a single bomber to enemy fighters in 200 escort bombing missions. . . . This record, historians believe, is unmatched by any other unit."

cited in *Tuskegee News* (Pride Edition), March 8, 1990, from *Excel Magazine*

The *Booker T. Washington (Tuskegee University Archives)*

Dedicating the *Booker T. Washington (Tuskegee University Archives)*

The base and Chief Anderson produced another first. . . . in Gen. "Chappie" Daniel James, a fighter pilot and Tuskegee alum, the Air Force's first black four-star general.

"In 1941 the Army still regarded all blacks as totally inferior to whites—somewhat less than human, and certainly incapable of contributing positively to its combat mission."

DAVIS,
Autobiography

Gen. Benjamin O. Davis *(Library of Congress)*

"When the Tuskegee Airmen arrived, Portia's home became a main gathering place for them and their dates, with Portia providing refreshments and of course the music."

HILL,
Booker T's Child

99TH PURSUIT WINGS

Hotter than a spitfire!

3 pounds chicken wings	2 garlic cloves, minced
4 teaspoons garlic powder	½ tablespoon fresh lemon juice
2 teaspoons onion powder	2 tablespoons chopped onion
3 teaspoons cayenne pepper	6 fresh jalapeño peppers, seeded and finely chopped
3 teaspoons Worcestershire sauce	1½ teaspoons dry mustard
1 teaspoon dry mustard	1 teaspoon Worcestershire sauce
1 onion, coarsely chopped	½ cup hot pepper (Red Devil or Louisiana) sauce
¼ cup vegetable oil	1 tablespoon cayenne pepper
2 cups all-purpose flour	
2 teaspoons cayenne pepper	
3¼ teaspoons seasoned salt	1 cup vegetable shortening
1 teaspoon onion powder	¼ cup butter
1 teaspoon garlic powder	

Wash wings. Separate chicken wings at joints; discard tips. In a large bowl, combine chicken and next 7 ingredients. Refrigerate and allow to marinate for at least 2 hours or preferably overnight. Remove chicken and discard marinade. Salt and pepper chicken to taste. Mix together flour, cayenne, seasoned salt, onion powder, and garlic powder. Coat wings and reserve excess flour. Refrigerate wings an additional hour to allow flour to set. In a processor combine garlic, lemon juice, chopped onion, jalapeño peppers, dry mustard, Worcestershire, hot pepper sauce, and cayenne pepper; blend until smooth, and set aside. In a large heavy skillet over medium heat, warm shortening and butter to 375 degrees F. Coat wings with reserved flour once more. Shake off excess flour, and fry wings until well done and golden brown on all sides, about 10 to 15 minutes. Allow cooked wings to drain on a warm, paper towel–lined platter. When all of the wings have been fried, remove oil from pan and, over a low flame, heat blended hot pepper sauce. Simmer over low heat for approximately 10 minutes. Serve hot sauce on the side with vegetable crudités, blue cheese or ranch dressing, and lots of ice-cold beer.

6 to 8 servings

GARLIC-LIME WINGS

3   pounds chicken wings
¾   teaspoon garlic powder
¼   teaspoon onion powder
¼   teaspoon cayenne pepper
7   garlic cloves, minced

1¼   teaspoons seasoned salt
⅓   cup olive oil
¾   cup fresh lime juice
     Garlic salt

Preheat oven to 375 degrees F. Wash chicken wings and separate at joints. Discard tips, or save them for some other use. In a large mixing bowl, combine the next 5 ingredients; add chicken wings, and rub spices into them. Add olive oil and lime juice. Refrigerate 2 or 3 hours or overnight. Season chicken with garlic salt to taste. Grill chicken until it is cooked through, 12 to 15 minutes on each side depending on temperature of grill, or bake at 400 degrees F. for 15 or 20 minutes or until done. To test for doneness, pierce the thickest part of the chicken with a fork. Juices will run clear when done. Broil under high heat 3 to 5 minutes to brown. Cover with aluminum foil and keep warm until ready to serve.

6 to 8 servings

EL PASO CHEESE DIP

1   pound ground round, browned
     and crumbled, drained of any
     fat
1   pound Velveeta
1   pound Mexican mild Velveeta
1   pound Mexican hot Velveeta
16   ounces cream cheese
1   cup sliced green onions

3   garlic cloves, minced
4   medium tomatoes, chopped
¼   cup chopped jalapeño peppers
2   4-ounce cans chopped black
     olives
12   ounces diced chilies
     Corn chips

Place all ingredients, except chips, in a Crockpot, or other slow cooker; set on low heat and stir occasionally. Serve warm with chips.

24 to 30 servings

Rear view of Booker T. Washington's home. Onions are clearly visible in the foreground.
(*Library of Congress*)

CAROLYN'S SURE-SHOT HOT SALSA

5	fresh tomatoes, chopped
1	medium onion, chopped
1½	teaspoons minced cilantro
8	garlic cloves, minced
½	teaspoon onion powder
¾	teaspoon garlic powder
¾	teaspoon salt
8 to 9	fresh jalapeño peppers, seeded and chopped
3	tablespoons red hot pepper sauce (for milder salsa use fewer peppers and less hot pepper sauce)
¼	teaspoon cayenne pepper
3	tablespoons lime juice
¼	cup plus 2 tablespoons olive oil Tortilla chips

Combine all of the above ingredients (except the chips) and refrigerate, preferably overnight. Serve with tortilla chips.

4 to 6 servings

Black Bean Salsa

1	16-ounce can black beans, drained and rinsed
2	cups seeded and chopped fresh tomatoes
½	cup chopped black olives
1	cup chopped onion
½ to 1½	tablespoons chopped cilantro, depending on taste
3	fresh jalapeño peppers, seeded and chopped
4	garlic cloves, minced
1	tablespoon fresh lemon juice
¼	teaspoon salt
¼	teaspoon ground cumin
¼	teaspoon ground pepper
2	tablespoons virgin olive oil
1½	cups grilled chicken breast, diced (optional)

Combine all ingredients and refrigerate at least 2 or 3 hours before serving.

10 servings

Guacamole Dip

4	ripe avocados
1	large tomato
1	teaspoon garlic powder
½	teaspoon onion powder
1½	tablespoons fresh lemon juice
⅛	teaspoon chili powder
½	teaspoon salt

Mash avocados until smooth. Chop tomato and add to avocados. Add remaining ingredients and mix well. Refrigerate until ready for use.

18 to 24 servings

HUMMUS BI TAHINI

3½ cups chickpeas, dried (or two
      15-ounce cans)
3   garlic cloves
1   teaspoon salt
½   teaspoon ground cumin
⅛   teaspoon sesame oil
⅓   cup olive oil
3   tablespoons sesame tahini
      (available at health food
      stores)

Juice of 3 to 4 lemons, strained
Chopped parsley and cayenne
      pepper, for garnish
Olive oil
Pita bread

If dried chickpeas are used, cook according to package directions. Drain chickpeas, rinse, and set aside. Mash garlic with salt; add to chickpeas and purée in blender. Add cumin, oils, tahini; blend. Gradually add lemon juice to taste. Mix to a fine, smooth paste. If the hummus is too thick, thin by adding a little cold water. Serve on a shallow plate. Decorate with chopped parsley and red pepper. Offer olive oil in a separate dish and pita bread for dipping.

12 to 24 servings

EGGPLANT DIP

There are many variations of this recipe in Africa and the Middle East. In Tunisia it is called eggplant ajlouke. There, this coarsely puréed vegetable dish is served as a first course. You may also know this dish as baba ghanouj, which, however, is less piquant, and has a smoother texture.

1   large eggplant
1   teaspoon sesame tahini
      (available at health food
      stores)
2   tablespoons minced onion
2   garlic cloves, peeled and minced

½   teaspoon salt
2½   tablespoons olive oil
4   tablespoons lemon juice
2   tablespoons chopped parsley
      Pita or rye bread

Cover eggplant with water, and simmer over medium heat until tender, approximately 20 to 30 minutes. Cool. Peel eggplant, and then mash. Add remaining ingredients except parsley and bread. Beat until smooth. Mound on a shallow dish and garnish with chopped parsley. Chill well. Serve with pieces of pita bread or flat pieces of rye bread

8 to 12 servings

CAVIAR DIP

½ cup heavy cream	3 hard-boiled eggs, chopped
3 tablespoons red caviar, drained	¼ cup minced chives
2 tablespoons chopped shallots	Toast rounds

Whip cream, then fold in caviar and chopped shallots. Place in a bowl and garnish edges with chopped egg and chives. Serve with small rounds of toast.

18 to 24 servings

HOT CLAM DIP

2 cups minced clams, drained (reserve ¼ cup of the juice)	¼ teaspoon onion powder
8 ounces cream cheese, softened	1 tablespoon Worcestershire sauce
½ cup crumbled feta cheese	2 teaspoons fresh lemon juice
¼ cup whipping cream	1 round crusty bread, at least 8 inches in diameter
⅛ teaspoon dry mustard	
¼ teaspoon seasoned salt	

Preheat oven to 250 degrees F. Cut off top of the bread and scoop out the inside. Reserve bread pieces for dipping. Combine all remaining ingredients and pour into bread shell. Replace top and tightly wrap in foil. Place wrapped bread in a pie plate, and bake for approximately 2½ hours. Serve hot with pieces of the scooped-out bread. If the bottom three-quarters of the bread remains wrapped in foil, the dip will stay hot for 1 hour.

8 to 12 servings

SMOKED OYSTER DIP

2 cups smoked oysters, drained, (oil reserved), and minced	¼ teaspoon Liquid Smoke
8 ounces cream cheese, softened	⅛ teaspoon dry mustard
	½ cup heavy cream, whipped

Combine all ingredients, including the oil. Refrigerate until ready to use. Serve with chips or vegetable crudités.

12 to 18 servings

SMOKED SALMON BALL

2 cans smoked oysters, drained, (reserve 1 tablespoon of the oil)	1 teaspoon Liquid Smoke
	¼ teaspoon freshly ground pepper
16 ounces cream cheese (do not use presoftened)	1 16-ounce can boneless, skinless salmon

Reserve several oysters for garnish. In a large bowl, mash together the cheese, Liquid Smoke, pepper, remaining oysters, and reserved oil. In a separate bowl, pick over the salmon, removing any stray bones or skin. Mash well, and add to the cream cheese mixture. Blend thoroughly; shape into a ball, and chill for 2 hours. Just before serving, lightly dust ball with coarsely ground pepper and garnish with the reserved oysters. Serve with crackers.

12 to 18 servings

SMOKED OYSTER LOG

2	cans smoked oysters, drained, (reserve 1 tablespoon of the oil)	¼	teaspoon Liquid Smoke
		2	tablespoons mayonnaise
12	ounces cream cheese (do not use presoftened)	½	teaspoon paprika
			Dash of Tabasco
		1	cup coarsely chopped pecans

Mash oysters with cream cheese. Add reserved oil, Liquid Smoke, mayonnaise, paprika, and Tabasco. Blend well, and chill for 2 hours. Shape into a log. Stripe log, candy-cane fashion, with aluminum foil. Roll log in chopped pecans. Chill again, and remove foil stripe prior to serving.

12 to 18 servings

" *As a contribution toward the worthy object of procuring physical nourishment as well as mental, a friend gave $100.00, stipulating that it should be used to buy a horse to work the land.' Lewis Adams, a former slave who was instrumental, along with George Campbell, a former slave owner, in bringing Washington to Tuskegee with the telegram message 'Booker T. Washington will suit us,' purchased the horse. According to Adams, he stretched the $100.00 to cover not only a 'good' horse, a secondhand lumber wagon, a plow, harness, and a sack of corn to feed the horse. . . . Dr. Wash-*

Booker T. Washington on horseback (*Library of Congress*)

ington warmly referred to the horse variously as 'blind, as lame, as broken down, and
as worn out.'... However, the horse enabled the students to start planting cabbages,
watermelon, corn, sweet potatoes, and sorghum. 'This they did with enthusiasm,
because it promised something to eat.' 'All the industries at Tuskegee have been started
in natural and logical order growing out of the needs of a community settlement....
We began with farming because we wanted something to eat....'"

WASHINGTON,
Up From Slavery

SOUPS AND SALADS

Soup is a comfort food that evokes strong memories. In early autumn when jewel-toned leaves began to fall, my mother would take out the soup pot. From then until winter's end the heady fragrance of my mother's soup simmering on the back burner of the stove welcomed me home from school and play. To this day this aroma makes me feel warm, safe, and loved.

NAVY BEAN SOUP

1	pound dried great northern beans	4	cups water
¼	cup bacon drippings	2	quarts chicken broth
2	medium onions, chopped	1	ham hock, washed
2	garlic cloves, minced		Salt and pepper to taste
1	bay leaf	2½	cups diced ham
			Chopped tomato for garnish

Place beans in a large colander and remove stones or other foreign objects. Rinse the beans with cold water; place them in a large bowl. Add sufficient water to cover by 3 inches. Soak overnight. Drain and rinse beans. Melt drippings in a 6-quart heavy pot over medium heat. Add onion, garlic, and bay leaf. Sauté until onion is soft; then add water, broth, and ham hock to the pot. Bring to a boil. Reduce heat to low, and simmer for 1 hour. Add beans with sufficient liquid to cover; simmer, uncovered, an hour longer. Cover pot and simmer an additional hour. Add water as necessary. Season to taste with salt and pepper. For a smoother soup, remove beans from pot when tender and process through a food processor. Return mixture to pot, add diced ham, and reheat. Ladle into soup bowls, and top each serving with some of the tomato.

4 to 6 servings

Dining Room *(Library of Congress)*

BLACK BEAN SOUP

1 pound dried black beans	6 cups beef broth
2 green bell peppers, chopped	2 14- to 16-ounce cans tomatoes, undrained and chopped
1 large yellow onion, chopped	8 cups water
4 garlic cloves, minced	½ tablespoon seasoned salt
2 fresh jalapeño peppers, chopped	Sour cream
3 bay leaves	Green onions, chopped
¼ cup olive oil	
2 ham hocks, washed	

Pick over beans, removing any foreign objects. In a large bowl, soak beans overnight in sufficient cold water to cover by 3 inches. In a 6-quart pot, sauté bell peppers, onion, garlic, jalapeños, and bay leaves in olive oil over medium-low heat. Be careful not to burn the garlic. Add ham hocks, broth, tomatoes, and water to the pot. Bring to a boil, and reduce heat to low, and cover. Rinse and drain the beans, and add them to the pot. If necessary, add additional water to cover beans by 3 inches. Add seasoned salt; cover pot, and cook on low heat for about an hour, until the beans are extremely tender and the liquid thickens. Garnish individual servings with a dollop of sour cream and green onions.

4 to 6 servings

Booker T. Washington met his first wife while teaching in Tinkersville. He encouraged her to return to Hampton, where she was previously enrolled as a student but dropped out for financial reasons. For two winters she taught school three miles from Malden, walking three miles each way to save money. In 1880 she was reinstated after settling her bill for $48.00. Washington helped her through Hampton, along with his brother John. For a time they were at Hampton together, she as a student, he as a teacher of the night class. It was at this time that they fell in love. However, on May 31, 1881, General Armstrong recommended Washington to serve as Tuskegee's first principal. Fanny remained at Hampton and graduated while Booker went to Tuskegee.

> *"During the summer of 1882, at the end of the first year's work of the school, I was married to Miss Fannie N. [Norton] Smith, of Malden, W. Va."*
>
> WASHINGTON,
> *Up From Slavery*

ISLAND SOUP

Salt and pepper
3 cups fresh okra
¼ cup bacon drippings
2 large onions, chopped fine
1 large green bell pepper, seeded and chopped
5 garlic cloves, chopped fine
½ cup diced ham
2 quarts chicken broth
2 bay leaves
½ teaspoon ground allspice
½ teaspoon ground cumin
½ teaspoon cinnamon
5 black peppercorns
Pinch of powdered saffron
½ teaspoon seasoned salt
2 tablespoons vegetable shortening
4 tablespoons all-purpose flour
1 16-ounce can tomatoes
1 pound lump crabmeat
2 pounds cleaned shrimp
1 pint oysters, with their liquid

Salt and pepper okra to taste. In a large pot, over medium heat, fry okra in bacon drippings. Add onions, bell pepper, garlic, and ham. Fry until onions are transparent. Add chicken broth and next 7 seasoning ingredients. In a separate frying pan, melt shortening over high heat. Add flour and stir until a reddish brown roux is formed; be careful not to allow roux to burn. Next, add the tomatoes with liquid, stir, and add this mixture to the soup pot.

Simmer uncovered for an hour. About 5 or 10 minutes prior to serving, add crabmeat, shrimp, and oysters.

4 to 6 servings

MRS. GLAZE'S HOLIDAY CHOWDER

Mr. and Mrs. Jackson Glaze owned and operated a small grocery store just outside Tuskegee's back gate. The kindly couple listened to the woes of, and fed, many hungry students. Mrs. Glaze, an accomplished matchmaker, was responsible for many marriages, including mine. If you were one of Mary Glaze's "chil'drun," you couldn't go into the store without her offering you a cold drink, a sandwich, or some of the dinner she cooked every day in the back of the store for herself and her husband, Jack. Together, they embodied the true spirit of Tuskegee and its "first chef," Felix Branum. After the holidays Mrs. Glaze always had some of this chowder waiting for the returning students.

Actually, it can be made at any time. The reason that it's called Holiday Chowder is that holidays are usually the time of year there is most likely to be a large poultry frame around.

1	poultry frame (turkey or roasting hen)		1	teaspoon onion powder
	Water or chicken broth, sufficient to cover frame		2	teaspoons seasoned salt
			1½	cups mixed peas and carrots
1	medium onion, diced		1	cup frozen corn
1	stalk celery, chopped		1	16-ounce can whole tomatoes
2	garlic cloves, chopped		2	cups cooked elbow macaroni or egg noodles
1	teaspoon garlic powder			

Bring water or broth and frame to a boil. Reduce heat. Add onion, celery, garlic, and seasonings; cook for 1½ hours or until meat separates from the frame. Periodically check soup, stir, and retrieve clean bones from the pot and discard. Add vegetables and cooked noodles. Reduce heat and allow vegetables and noodles to heat through. Serve with J.R.'s Skillet Corn Bread, or Corn Sticks.

6 to 8 servings

SWEET POTATO SOUP

1	medium onion, sliced thin		2	large russet potatoes, peeled and sliced thin
½	tablespoon minced garlic			
2½	tablespoons butter		1	cup light cream
1	cup minced celery		¼	cup thinly sliced green onions
¼	teaspoon ground cumin			Salt and pepper
4	cups chicken broth			
3	large sweet potatoes, peeled and sliced thin			

In a medium saucepan, over medium heat, sauté onion and garlic in butter. Add celery and cumin and allow to cook an additional 2 minutes. Add broth and potatoes; bring to a boil. Reduce heat to medium-low, cover, and simmer an additional 25 to 30 minutes or until potatoes are tender. Purée potatoes, add cream, and simmer over low heat. If necessary, thin with water or additional chicken stock. Season with salt and pepper to taste. Ladle soup into bowls and garnish with green onions.

4 to 6 servings

CREAM OF PEANUT SOUP

¼ cup chopped celery	¼ teaspoon salt
1 medium onion, chopped fine	⅛ teaspoon cayenne pepper
¼ cup butter	1 cup light cream
2 teaspoons flour	¼ cup coarsely ground, skinless
2 quarts chicken broth	unsalted peanuts
1 cup creamy peanut butter	

In a large saucepan, over low heat, sauté celery and onion in melted butter until onion is transparent. Add flour and blend until lump free. Slowly add chicken broth, continue to stir, and bring to a boil. Blend in the peanut butter. Add spices and simmer approximately 15 minutes. Just prior to serving, stir in cream and garnish individual servings with ground peanuts.

4 to 6 servings

CRAB BISQUE

2	tablespoons butter		¼	teaspoon ground thyme
1¼	cups finely chopped yellow onion		4	cups clam juice
1	cup finely chopped celery		½	cup peeled and diced russet potato
1	cup chopped red bell pepper		¾	cup light cream
1	small bay leaf		2	tablespoons scotch whisky
1½	teaspoons Seafood Seasoning (page 66)		1	pound lump crabmeat
	Salt to taste			Salt and pepper
½	teaspoon cayenne pepper			Chopped chives for garnish

Over medium heat, melt butter in a heavy medium-size pot. Add onion, celery, red bell pepper, bay leaf, and seasonings. Reduce heat to low, cover, and cook for 5 minutes. Stir a couple of times to prevent sticking. Add clam juice and diced potato; bring to a boil. Reduce heat, partially cover pot, and simmer until the potato is very tender. Purée soup in blender until smooth. Return to pot; add cream, scotch, and crabmeat. Season with salt and pepper to taste. Garnish individual servings with chopped chives.

4 to 6 servings

SORREL SOUP*

We hope every person who likes something new, novel, delicious, nourishing and appetizing will try this soup. Thoroughly clean and wash about 2 quarts of the leaves, boil slowly until tender (preferably in a porcelain or granite ware vessel); rub through a sieve, add your favorite seasoning and three cups of soup stock to it; thicken with

*Recipe titles followed by an asterisk are just as George Washington Carver wrote them in his bulletins and reports to farmers.

one tablespoonful of butter and one of flour rubbed together, and stir this into a teacupful of boiling hot milk. Add to the soup stirring it vigorously to prevent curdling. Let boil up and serve at once with croutons or toasted crackers.

[4 servings]

CARVER,

Nature's Garden

George Washington Carver was born to a slave woman named Mary. Shortly after his birth he and his mother were kidnapped by slave raiders. Eventually, Moses and Susan Carver recovered George and raised him and his brother Jim as members of their family. Although George's fragile health prevented him from performing heavy labor, he was taught the domestic arts of cooking, sewing, housekeeping, and laundering.

After receiving a B.A. from Iowa State in 1894 and an M.S. in November 1896, Booker T. Washington offered him a position at Tuskegee. On the way to the school he observed signs of soil erosion and mineral depletion. His early suspicions were confirmed when he saw stunted cotton plants growing in the field. He knew that while cotton may have been king, it left the soil a pauper as it drained it of its minerals.

The next spring, Carver instructed his students to plant cowpeas instead of cotton. At that time cowpeas were used as cow feed and had no cash value. The students were stunned. Carver explained how the cowpea replenished the soil. When the cowpeas were harvested, he invited the students to a dinner of meatloaf, pancakes, and a potato casserole—all made of cowpeas. The next year they planted sweet potatoes, followed by peanuts. They experimented in the lab finding hundreds of new uses for the sweet potato and the peanut that created markets for these crops and saved the South's faltering economy. And when they did plant cotton again, it was strong, full cotton.

During his career Carver made approximately three hundred products from the peanut. In addition to inventing and experimenting, most of his time was spent teaching. The agriculture program rapidly grew and gained a national reputation. In later years, he managed the Institute farm, as well as its livestock herd, poultry yard, orchard, agricultural department, and experiment station. He continued to experiment, publish bulletins and articles, and accept public speaking engagements. Despite the many demands on him, he always found time for demonstration work among the local farmers and homemakers.

DR. CARVER'S DANDELION SALAD*

This is the ordinary dandelion of our dooryard, field and road sides, with which we are more or less familiar. It is very tender and delicious now (February 20), and may be served in a variety of appetizing ways (use leaves only).

   A simple plain and appetizing salad may be made thus:

1 pint of finely shredded young dandelion leaves	1 tablespoon of minced parsley
1 medium sized onion, finely chopped	1 tablespoon of sugar (can be left out)
2 small radishes, finely chopped	Salt and pepper to taste

Moisten thoroughly with weak vinegar or mayonnaise, mix, place in salad dish and garnish with slices of hard boiled egg and pickled beets. This is only one of the many delicious and appetizing salads that will suggest themselves to the resourceful housewife.

   Aside from the dandelion's value for food, it is well known and highly prized for its many curative properties.

[4 servings]

CARVER,
Nature's Garden

DR. CARVER'S ALFALFA SALAD*

The young, tender leaves and stems are especially good when mixed with other greens, and especially piquant and appetizing made into a salad, thus: Wash and prepare the alfalfa similar to that of lettuce, garnish the whole with shredded onion, radishes, pickled beets, carrots, etc. Serve with mayonnaise or French dressing. This salad lends itself to an almost endless variety of artistic combinations in the way of ribbons, spots, layers, jellied etc. The nutritional value of alfalfa is too well known to need further discussion here.

CARVER,
Nature's Garden

CREAMY CUCUMBER AND ONION SALAD

3	cucumbers, peeled and sliced	½	teaspoon sugar
1	medium Bermuda onion, peeled and sliced thin	½	teaspoon coarsely ground pepper
½	teaspoon salt	1	tablespoon fresh lemon juice
1	cup sour cream	¼	cup chopped chives
½	cup milk	2	tablespoons chopped parsley

In a serving bowl, arrange cucumbers and onion. In a separate bowl, mix remaining ingredients and pour over salad. Lightly toss and refrigerate until ready to serve.

4 to 6 servings

DILLED CUCUMBER SALAD

2 1-pound unwaxed cucumbers,
    peeled and thinly sliced
1 onion, sliced thin
½ teaspoon salt
⅓ cup sour cream
½ teaspoon sugar

3 tablespoons fresh lime juice
2 tablespoons minced fresh
    dillweed
½ cup thinly sliced radishes
1 tablespoon chopped fresh
    chives

Peel and slice cucumbers and onion, then salt. Place salted cucumbers and onion in a paper towel–lined colander to absorb excess moisture. In a serving bowl, combine sour cream, sugar, lime juice, and dillweed, stirring until smooth. Add cucumber mixture and radishes; toss gently. Cover and chill 1 hour. Garnish with chopped chives just before serving.

6 to 8 servings

SOUR CREAM CUCUMBER SALAD

2 cucumbers
2 shallots
½ cup sour cream
¼ cup vinegar

¾ teaspoon salt
⅛ teaspoon paprika
2 tablespoons sugar

Cut cucumbers and shallots into thin slices. Combine remaining ingredients in a serving bowl and mix well. Add cucumbers and shallots, stir to coat with sour cream mixture, and refrigerate.

4 to 6 servings

Hoeing *(Library of Congress)*

GEORGE W. CARVER SALAD

For many years Dr. Carver included wild vegetables in his own diet and espoused the many nutritional and health benefits to be derived from nature's garden. In March of 1942, it was expected that the war effort would result in shortages of fresh vegetables on the home front. In response to this concern Dr. Carver published Bulletin No. 43, *Nature's Garden for Victory and Peace,* in hopes that "everyone [would] get acquainted with the wonderful food and medicinal value of these wild vegetables and make them a permanent part of their diet. . . ." This salad is named in honor of this health-conscious scientist.

¼ cup Belgian endive

2 cups Bibb lettuce

1 cup oak leaf lettuce

12 spinach leaves

½ cup chives, chopped

¼ cup mint, chopped

¼ cup radicchio

1 carrot, thinly sliced

2 hard-boiled eggs, peeled and quartered

¼ cup red clover flower heads

¼ cup violet heads

¼ cup primrose heads

Herbed Vinaigrette Dressing, recipe follows

Rinse greens and herbs with cold water. Using a soft cotton towel, pat greens until almost dry, and then wrap in a towel and refrigerate until chilled crisp. Dry greens completely and transfer to a large bowl, add carrot, and arrange egg quarters on top. Drizzle with Herb Vinaigrette Dressing, and toss lightly to coat. Just prior to serving, strew salad with flower heads. According to Dr. Carver, "clover flower heads have held first place in delicate and fancy salads for many years. Serve in mixed salads or separately as fancy dictates."

8 to 12 servings

HERB VINAIGRETTE DRESSING

⅓   cup water
⅓   cup cider vinegar
¼   teaspoon salt
¼   teaspoon black pepper
⅛   teaspoon cayenne pepper

⅔   cup virgin olive oil
2   teaspoons minced fresh chives
1   teaspoon minced fresh chervil
1   teaspoon minced fresh parsley

Combine ingredients in a suitably sized cruet, shake, and drizzle on the George W. Carver Salad, preceding recipe. Toss and serve immediately.

1⅓ cups

"Professor Washington enjoyed gardening and raised particularly large and succulent onions, which Dr. Carver coveted for himself. Returning once from an early morning walk, he dropped in to see how the principal's garden was coming along. Mr. Washington was presumably at his office. Dr. Carver swiped three onions and was just leaving with his booty when he beheld Mr. Washington entering the gate. 'I didn't mean

for you to see me,' he grinned, and received an answering grin. As a matter of fact, he had a fair exchange to offer, because he had been out gathering choice wild vegetables for his friend, whose dietary [sic] was limited."

HOLT,
George Washington Carver

SLICED TOMATO AND ONION SALAD

7	vine-ripened tomatoes, thinly sliced	3	medium onions, thinly sliced

Arrange vegetables on a serving platter, alternating tomatoes and onions. Sprinkle with Herb Vinaigrette Dressing (preceding recipe) and refrigerate at least 1 hour prior to serving.

6 to 8 servings

MIXED GARDEN SALAD AND DRESSING

1	head Bibb lettuce	2	cups cherry tomatoes, halved
1	head Belgian endive	2	shallots, sliced thin
1	small head iceberg lettuce	2	tablespoons chopped chives
2	cups tender spinach leaves	2	hard-boiled eggs, chopped

Wash the greens in ice water, drain, and pat dry. Tear greens, assemble salad, and place in the refrigerator to crisp while you make the dressing.

GARDEN FRESH DRESSING

2 large garlic cloves, crushed
⅔ cup olive oil
⅓ cup tarragon vinegar
1 teaspoon garlic powder
1 teaspoon onion powder
1½ teaspoons seasoned salt

¼ teaspoon paprika
⅛ teaspoon cayenne pepper
¼ teaspoon freshly ground black
    pepper
⅓ cup + 2 tablespoons water

In a cruet or jar, combine all of the above ingredients, cover, and shake well. Pour over salad immediately before serving.

8 to 12 servings

Tuskegee gardener *(Library of Congress)*

OLD-TIME POTATO SALAD

3	large potatoes		3	tablespoons vinegar
1	large Bermuda onion, sliced thin		1	garlic clove, finely minced
5 to 7	sprigs fresh parsley		½	teaspoon salt
¼	cup olive oil		¼	teaspoon ground black pepper
			2	tablespoons sugar

Boil potatoes until soft, remove from water, and cool. In a large bowl, slice potatoes into ¼-inch-thick slices. Alternate with sliced onion on a platter. Mince 3 sprigs of the parsley. In a small bowl, mix together oil, vinegar, garlic, minced parsley, sugar, salt, and black pepper. Pour mixture over potatoes and onions, then toss lightly. Season to taste with additional salt and pepper and refrigerate. This salad is at its zenith when refrigerated overnight. Garnish with remaining sprigs of parsley prior to serving.

6 to 8 servings

CREAMY POTATO SALAD

10 to 12	large red potatoes		1½	teaspoons salt
1	cup heavy cream		1	cup thinly sliced green onions or chives
3	tablespoons cider vinegar			
1½	tablespoons vegetable oil			

In salted water, boil whole potatoes in their jackets. Allow potatoes to cool just enough to handle without burning your fingers. While potatoes are cooling, combine remaining ingredients in a large bowl. Quarter warm potatoes, add to the dressing, toss lightly, and serve.

About 12 servings

DOWN-HOME POTATO SALAD FOR A CROWD

10 to 12	russet potatoes		⅓	cup + 2 tablespoons sweet relish
2	large celery ribs, minced		1	tablespoon dill relish
1	medium green bell pepper, diced		⅛	teaspoon celery seed
1	small onion, minced		⅛	teaspoon dry mustard
8 to 10	hard-boiled eggs, chopped		⅛	teaspoon paprika
2	cups mayonnaise			Seasoned salt to taste

Place potatoes in a large pot and cover with cold water. Bring to a boil over high heat. Reduce heat to moderate-high, and cook, covered, until tender, approximately 20 to 30 minutes. Drain, and set aside to cool. Peel and dice. In a large bowl, combine celery, bell pepper, and onion. Add potatoes, then eggs, mayonnaise, and seasonings. Adjust salad's moisture and seasoning to taste. If dry, add more mayonnaise. Mix gently, and refrigerate at least 3 hours prior to serving or, preferably, overnight.

18 to 20 servings

FESTIVAL SALAD

3	pounds red potatoes, unpeeled and scrubbed		¾	cup olive oil
¼	cup chopped green onions, including tops		¼	cup fresh lemon juice
½	cup chopped red bell pepper		½	cup minced parsley
½	cup chopped yellow bell pepper		1	garlic clove, minced
			⅛	teaspoon celery seed
			½	teaspoon seasoned salt

Place potatoes in a large pot and cover with cold water. Bring to a boil over high heat. Reduce heat to moderate-high, and cook, covered, until tender, approximately 20 to 30 minutes. Drain and set aside to cool. Quarter potatoes in a large bowl; add green onions and peppers. In a separate bowl, combine olive oil, lemon juice, parsley, garlic, celery seed, and seasoned salt, and whisk to blend. Pour over salad, toss lightly, and serve immediately.

8 to 10 servings

POTATO AND HAM SALAD

2	large baking potatoes	1	cup beef broth
½	cup cubed smoked ham	¼	cup chopped Bermuda onion
1	tablespoon chopped parsley	1	tablespoon sugar
¾	cup sliced green onions	¼	teaspoon pepper
¼	teaspoon celery seed	¼	cup cider vinegar
½	teaspoon minced fresh basil	1½	tablespoons all-purpose flour
½	teaspoon minced fresh thyme		

Boil potatoes until tender. Remove from water, cool, and peel. In a large bowl, slice potatoes into ¼-inch-thick slices. Add chopped ham and next 5 ingredients. Gently mix ingredients together. Combine beef broth and next 3 ingredients in a saucepan. Bring to a boil, reduce heat, and simmer 5 minutes. In a small bowl, whisk together vinegar and flour until smooth. Add this mixture to beef broth mixture. Continue to simmer, stirring an additional 2 minutes. Pour over potatoes and toss lightly. Serve at room temperature.

4 to 6 servings

COLE SLAW

5 cups grated cabbage	½ cup mayonnaise
2 cups grated carrots	2 teaspoons sugar
½ teaspoon celery seed	½ teaspoon onion powder
¼ cup sour cream	½ teaspoon seasoned salt
½ cup table cream	

In a large serving bowl, combine the first 2 ingredients. In a separate mixing bowl, combine the remaining ingredients; add to cabbage mixture. Coat thoroughly, and refrigerate at least 2 or 3 hours prior to serving.

5 servings

CREAMY COLE SLAW

1 small head cabbage, shredded fine	⅓ cup mayonnaise
2 medium carrots, shredded fine	2 tablespoons sugar
½ tablespoon coarsely grated onion	1 teaspoon salt
	⅛ teaspoon celery seed
¼ cup + 2 tablespoons heavy cream	1 tablespoon cider vinegar

Combine vegetables in a bowl. In a separate bowl, combine remaining ingredients, pour over salad, and toss lightly.

Serves 12

MAIN DISHES

The aromas of a roasting turkey or a Sunday pot roast are the fragrances that make a house a home. My fondest memories of my early years involve great times and great meals. When I left home to attend Tuskegee, I met new friends, married, and created new traditions. I also carried with me warm embers from my mother's kitchen. I know now that home is where the hearth is.

"Despite a winter of hardship and discomfort, students flocked to the school in increasing numbers. When summer came, Washington set the students to constructing a new three-story wood frame building for the newcomers. 'They were not skilled carpenters, but in spite of the mistakes the frame walls rose steadily, and in the room set aside to be used as a chapel the four teachers and one hundred and fifty students were able to hold their Thanksgiving service. A second service of thanksgiving was held at Christmas; the last payment had been made, and the land and all that was on it belonged to them.' "

HOLT,
George Washington Carver

Refreshment stand *(Library of Congress)*

ROAST TURKEY AND GIBLET GRAVY

ROAST TURKEY

1	18- to 24-pound USDA grade A turkey		1	teaspoon ground sage
2	tablespoons seasoned salt		¾	teaspoon ground paprika
1	tablespoon poultry seasoning		1	large onion, quartered
2	teaspoons ground thyme		1	green bell pepper, seeded and quartered
2	teaspoons meat tenderizer		1	navel orange, quartered
1½	teaspoons garlic powder		1	apple, seeded and quartered
1½	teaspoons onion powder		2	stalks celery with leaves, halved
1½	teaspoons ground pepper		1	cup orange juice

Preheat oven to 325 degrees F. Take turkey from its packaging. Remove giblets and neck; set aside for the Giblet Gravy, recipe follows. Rinse the bird under cold running water. Pat the bird dry, then place it, breast side up, in a roasting pan. Mix together salt and seasonings, and then thoroughly season the bird, inside and out, with the mixture. Don't forget the neck cavity. Fill the neck and body cavity with the cut-up vegetables, fruit, and orange juice. Fold wings under the body and tie legs together. Cover the breast with a piece of aluminum foil and roast approximately 15 minutes per pound. Baste about every 30 minutes, and remove the foil after approximately 1 hour to allow the bird to brown. Check often, and replace the foil should the bird become too brown. Serve with dressing, Giblet Gravy, below, Sweet Potato Casserole, fresh collard greens, Homemade Cranberry Cups, and Butter Rolls.

16 to 18 servings

GIBLET GRAVY

1	quart chicken broth		¼	cup chopped celery
1	teaspoon seasoned salt		¼	cup bacon drippings or lard
½	teaspoon garlic powder			Drippings from turkey
	Turkey giblets and neck		1	cup milk
½	cup chopped onion		¼	cup all-purpose flour
½	cup chopped green bell pepper			

In a medium saucepan, bring chicken broth, salt, and garlic powder to boil; add washed giblets and neck. Reduce heat and simmer for 30 to 45 minutes. Remove giblets and neck from broth, allow to cool, chop, and set giblets and broth aside. In a separate pan, sauté onion, bell pepper, and celery in bacon drippings, until onion becomes almost transparent. Stir to prevent sticking. After removing cooked turkey from pan to a serving platter, place the roasting pan over two burners and deglaze with reserved giblet broth. Pour pan contents into a medium saucepan; degrease; add milk and cook over medium heat. Add sautéed vegetables and chopped giblets. Add flour and stir constantly with a wire whisk until gravy boils, about 2 minutes. Use additional flour-water paste or milk to adjust the consistency as desired. Serve with Roast Turkey, preceding recipe, and Southern Corn Bread Dressing.

4 to 6 servings

MAMA ELLEN'S GIBLET GRAVY (WITHOUT PAN DRIPPINGS)

2	quarts chicken broth		1½	pounds giblets
2	teaspoons seasoned salt		1	cup chopped onions
1	teaspoon rubbed sage		½	cup chopped green bell pepper
1	teaspoon garlic powder		¼	cup chopped celery
½	teaspoon coarsely ground pepper		1	cup water
½	teaspoon ground thyme		½	cup all-purpose flour

In a medium saucepan, bring chicken broth, seasoned salt, sage, garlic powder, pepper, and thyme to a boil. Reduce heat and add giblets. Simmer over low heat, covered, for 1 hour. Remove giblets from broth; allow to cool and chop. Return chopped giblets to broth, add vegetables, and heat to medium. In a separate bowl, mix together water and flour to form a smooth, thin paste. Slowly add flour paste to broth mixture. Cook, stirring constantly, until gravy boils, about 2 minutes.

About 12 servings

QUAIL THE SOUTHERN WAY

After World War I, returning black veterans were not admitted to white institutions. Tuskegee, in exchange for one dollar, presented the federal government with four hundred acres of land on which to build Tuskegee's veterans' hospital. When Vice President Coolidge came to Tuskegee to dedicate the land, trustee Charles Wickersham was assigned to escort him. Wickersham discovered that the vice president was not very talkative, and he was concerned that something was wrong. He decided to see if the guesthouse cook was aware of any problems. After expressing his concern, the cook replied, "Well, Mr. Wickersham, there's two things: I got quail fixed up the southern way. And if that don't work, wait till he sees Professor Carver." Although we have no record of exactly what Cook meant by "quail . . . the southern way," the following recipe, a West African adaptation for guinea hen, popular at the time, may well have been used.

8	plump quail		½	cup all-purpose flour
2	teaspoons salt		3	tablespoons bacon drippings
½	teaspoon black pepper		1	small onion, chopped fine
½	teaspoon dry mustard		2	garlic cloves, crushed
¼	teaspoon garlic powder		2	cups chicken broth
⅛	teaspoon cayenne pepper		2	tablespoons all-purpose flour

Clean the birds. Combine salt, pepper, mustard, garlic powder, and cayenne pepper, and rub into the cavities of the birds. Truss the birds. Lightly coat the birds with the ½ cup flour, taking care to shake off excess. Melt drippings in a large casserole (you may require 2 casseroles) with a tight-fitting lid. Add onion, garlic, and quail to the pan. Over medium heat, sauté until delicately brown on all sides, turning frequently. Add chicken broth, cover tightly, and simmer over low heat for 40 to 45 minutes or until tender when tested with a fork. Do not overcook or birds will fall into pieces. Remove quail from casserole; thicken juice with the 2 tablespoons of flour to form a gravy. Serve 2 birds to each guest with gravy and wild or white rice.

4 servings

At the end of the of the first year, a ceremony marked the day of the school's final exercises. At the A.M.E. church, class recitations began at ten o'clock and lasted an hour and a half. After the ceremony, dinner was served picnic style on the grounds. Visitors brought their baskets with them.

SUNDAY POT ROAST

1	5-pound rump roast
1	tablespoon brown sugar
2	teaspoons garlic powder
2	teaspoons onion powder
1½	teaspoons seasoned salt
1	teaspoon pepper
3	tablespoons vegetable shortening
1	large onion, chopped
2	stalks celery, sliced
1	green bell pepper, seeded and chopped
3	garlic cloves, chopped
2	cups water
¼	teaspoon dried basil
¼	teaspoon dried oregano
1	bay leaf
2	cups whole mushrooms, cleaned and stemmed
1	cup cold water
3	tablespoons all-purpose flour
2	cups beef broth

Wash roast and pat dry. Mix together the next 5 ingredients and use to season the roast. If possible, refrigerate overnight. Melt shortening in a deep, heavy pot over medium-high heat. When a drop of water can dance in the pot, add the roast and brown on all sides. The sugar helps the meat to brown to a nice rich color. Remove the meat from the pan and add the onion, celery, bell pepper, and chopped garlic. Sauté lightly and return the roast to the pan. Add 2 cups water, basil, oregano, and bay leaf to pot. Cover and simmer over low heat for 3 or 4 hours. Add more water as required to keep the roast from sticking. Approximately 15 minutes before the roast is done, add mushrooms and allow to cook an additional 15 minutes. When the roast is done, remove it from the pot. Retrieve ½ cup of juice, and add to it the cold water and the flour, mixing well to ensure there are no lumps. Return this mixture and beef broth to the pot and stir over low heat until gravy boils, about 2 minutes. Thicken gravy by adding more flour-water paste. Thin gravy by adding water. Allow roast to cool, slice thin, and return to hot gravy and reheat. Serve with Creamy Mashed Potatoes, Ham-Flavored Green Beans, Garden Salad, or Pickled Beets, and Church Social Yeast Biscuits. May be sliced thin and served cold with horseradish sauce at a picnic.

12 to 15 servings

GLAZED COUNTRY HAM

Always a frugal man, Carver encouraged financial independence and discouraged the farmers from shopping at the high-priced plantation commissaries. According to him, "[to] be happy, the farmer must raise his living at home." Professor Carver described how he walked in unexpectedly on one family, just in time for supper. Supper consisted of ham and eggs raised on the farm, homemade butter, canned fruit, and syrup and biscuits made from flour which had been purchased from the surplus.

1	10- to 15-pound Virginia or Smithfield country ham		Whole cloves sufficient to garnish ham	
10	whole cloves	¾	cup honey	
10	whole allspice	¼	cup molasses	
5	whole peppercorns	¼	cup cornmeal	
1	cinnamon stick	½	cup brown sugar	
2	apples, peeled and quartered	3	tablespoons dry mustard	
2	bay leaves	½	teaspoon ground allspice	
¼	cup brown sugar	¼	teaspoon ground cloves	
1	quart apple cider	⅛	teaspoon ground cinnamon	
½	navel orange			

Cover ham with cold water and soak 24 to 36 hours before cooking. Using a stiff brush, scrub away any mold from ham surface. Discard soaking water; rinse ham and place it in a large roasting pan. Add whole cloves, next 7 ingredients, and cold water to cover; bring to a boil over high heat. Reduce heat to low; cover and simmer 20 to 25 minutes per pound or until the ham reaches an internal temperature of 150 degrees F. Add the apple cider and orange during the last ½ hour of cooking. Drain liquid from ham. Remove skin while ham is still warm, leaving fat intact. Trim excess fat, and score in a diamond pattern. Place a whole clove in the center of each diamond. Combine honey and molasses; brush all over ham. Combine cornmeal with next 5 ingredients and use to dust the ham. Place ham in preheated 425 degree F. oven long enough to glaze. Slice very thin. May be served warm or cold.

10 to 12 servings

FRIED HAM WITH RED-EYE GRAVY

Cured or country ham, sliced ¼ to ½ inch thick

½ cup hot water
¼ cup hot strong coffee

Score fat around ham edges to prevent them from curling while cooking. If ham is very salty, cover with water and simmer briefly, about 3 minutes, turning frequently. Discard cooking water, cover with fresh water, and continue to simmer until water evaporates. Allow meat to fry over moderate heat, turning several times until brown on each side. Remove from pan and keep warm. There should be a reddish-brown glaze on the bottom of the pan. Add hot water and coffee to the pan, stirring constantly and cooking until gravy turns red. Serve with red-eye gravy, grits, and hot Baking Powder Biscuits.

"[The annual fair had a humble beginning in 1898. But each fall of the year thereafter, they gathered in the old battalion ground.] On Friday morning could be seen farmers from all sections of the county making their way to the fair bringing turkeys, chickens, geese, various kinds of corn, sugar cane . . . and other farm products for exhibit. The wives of these farmers were bringing canned fruits, wines, jellies and fancy needlework."

Tuskegee Student Newspaper,
October 27, 1906

"On oxcarts and mule wagons stretching out a quarter of a mile, they rode in the night before and during the early morning—handkerchiefed-headed aunties and gingham gowned young women; old men smoking their corncobs, young men in their best,

though often their coats were many patched; excited children with big eyes gleaming from their dark little faces. At such times the roads leading to Tuskegee were never empty and the dust never settled."

HOLT,
George Washington Carver

"In the battalion ground many of the farmers spent the night twining paper ribbons on the spokes of their wagon wheels, setting candy-striped poles in the corners, fastening on their tallest stalks of corn. . . . In the morning they gathered outside the pavilion, which had been freshly sprinkled with sawdust from the mill and decorated with branches of longleaf pine, partly to enliven the bare, drab boards and also to keep out the weather, February weather being uncertain. From the smooth needles rain slid quickly and soundlessly to . . . the earth. At twelve came recess and dinner, and the barbecued oxen and hogs and sheep were washed down with gallons of coffee and red lemonade."

HOLT,
George Washington Carver

"A delicious aroma of roast pig drifting on the campus air met them, and light glowed red from the barbecue pit, where student cooks performed all night at the savory task of basting."

HOLT,
George Washington Carver

ROAST SUCKLING PIG

1	10- to 15-pound suckling pig (about 1 pound per person), split in half and prepared by butcher for roasting	1¼	teaspoons freshly ground black pepper
10	large garlic cloves	¼	teaspoon cayenne pepper
1	tablespoon salt	½	cup fresh lime juice
1½	teaspoons onion powder	½	cup fresh lemon juice
¼	teaspoon rubbed sage	¾	cup orange juice
⅛	teaspoon ground cloves		Hickory chips
			Charcoal
			Barbecue sauce

A day ahead, wash the pig inside and out under cold running water and pat dry with a clean cloth. Mash the garlic and combine with the salt, onion powder, sage, cloves, and ground peppers to form a paste. Place the pig in a large pan and rub inside and out with the garlic paste. Combine lemon, lime, and orange juices and pour over the pig. Cover with aluminum foil and refrigerate overnight. Soak hickory chips in water and begin heating coals in an open-pit grill approximately ½ hour before cooking. Spread chips evenly over coals. Place the grating approximately 12 inches above the burning coals. Wrap the pig's ears and tail in aluminum foil to prevent burning. Place a small ball of aluminum foil in each eye socket to maintain the shape. Place pig, opened flat and skin side down, on the grill. Cook, allowing 25 minutes for each pound of meat, and turn every 25 minutes for even cooking. During the last 2 hours of cooking, remove the foil from the ears and tail, and baste with barbecue sauce. Test for doneness by checking the pig's inner cavity for any pink spots. When the pig is done to an internal temperature of 185 to 190 degrees F. and juices run clear when the thigh is pierced with a fork, remove the meat to a large platter. Join the pig halves together and allow to rest 15 to 20 minutes before carving. Meanwhile, place cherries or cranberries in the eye sockets. Place toothpicks around the neck at intervals, and attach clusters of grapes.

10 to 15 servings

SOUTHERN BARBECUE

Timing is everything when it comes to that down-home, succulently tasty, finger-lick'n good, fight for the last piece, southern barbecue. It's very important to marinate the meat well, at least 24 hours. Aunt Bay Bay's Barbecue Marinade, below, is the very best. Next you want to cook your meat on a very slow fire, using hickory chips. I prefer using a covered grill so that I can keep the smoke circulating around the meat. After I finish grilling the meat, I place it in large resealable plastic bags and refrigerate overnight. The next day I remove the meat from the bags and reheat it in a covered roaster by placing it in a warm (lowest setting) oven for about an hour. This method takes a little extra time; however, the results are well worth the extra effort.

"At seven or eight in the evening all climbed into their carts and wagons and buggies again and started, many of them on another all-night ride for home."

HOLT,
George Washington Carver

AUNT BAY BAY'S BARBECUE MARINADE

½	cup vegetable oil
2	bay leaves, crushed
1	teaspoon curry powder
½	teaspoon dried basil
⅛	teaspoon marjoram
⅛	teaspoon savory spice
¼	teaspoon dried thyme
½	teaspoon turmeric
1¼	teaspoons lemon pepper
⅛	teaspoon ground nutmeg
1¾	teaspoons seasoned salt
1	tablespoon paprika
1	teaspoon ground cumin
¾	teaspoon garlic powder
½	teaspoon onion powder
¼	teaspoon cayenne pepper
1	lemon
1	large onion, sliced
7	garlic cloves, minced
3½	cups water
1	red bell pepper, seeded and chopped
5	fresh jalapeño peppers, sliced
2	tablespoons Liquid Smoke
1	tablespoon vinegar

Pour oil into large bowl. Add dry spices and garlic. Add remaining ingredients and mix well. Warm oil for 30 seconds in microwave or on top of the stove. The warmth enhances the release of the spices' flavor. Add meat to bowl and marinate overnight. Reserve marinade to use in making Aunt Bay Bay's Barbecue Sauce.

About 4 cups

AUNT BAY BAY'S BARBECUE SAUCE

	Aunt Bay Bay's Barbecue Marinade, preceding recipe	½	teaspoon ground allspice
1¼	cups tomato juice	½	teaspoon ground cloves
2	tomatoes, quartered	¼	teaspoon celery seed
¼	cup Worcestershire sauce	¾	teaspoon dry mustard
3	tablespoons Liquid Smoke	4½	teaspoons paprika
2½	cups malt liquor beer	1	teaspoon lemon pepper
½	cup hot pepper sauce	2	lemon slices
2	tablespoons maple syrup	1½	teaspoons cayenne pepper
		4	tablespoons cornstarch

In a medium pot, combine Aunt Bay Bay's Barbecue Marinade and all other ingredients except the cornstarch. Over high heat, bring this mixture to a boil. Reduce heat to low and simmer 1 hour. Place in a blender or processor to purée vegetables; then return mixture to pot to thicken. Combine cornstarch and ½ cup water, add to sauce, stir, and simmer 10 minutes longer. This sauce is lip-smacking, bread-sopping good.

About 2 quarts

DEVILED CRAB

¼ cup onion, chopped fine

¼ cup minced green bell pepper

3 tablespoons minced celery

½ cup melted butter

1¼ pounds fresh lump crabmeat, well drained

1 teaspoon Seafood Seasoning, recipe follows

¼ cup cream

1 large egg, beaten

2 tablespoons all-purpose flour

1 tablespoon minced fresh jalapeño pepper (optional)

1 teaspoon Tabasco sauce

¼ teaspoon onion powder

⅛ teaspoon garlic powder

1 cup dry bread crumbs

½ cup vegetable shortening

Over medium heat, sauté onion, bell pepper, and celery in ¼ cup of the butter until tender. Add crabmeat and Seafood Seasoning. Mix well. Remove from heat and combine all remaining ingredients except bread crumbs, shortening, and remaining butter. Shape into hush puppy–like cylinders. Coat with bread crumbs and chill at least 1 hour. Cook in shortening and remaining butter over medium-high heat until golden on all sides, approximately 5 to 8 minutes.

6 or 8 servings

SEAFOOD SEASONING

2 tablespoons celery salt

1 tablespoon ground bay leaves

1 tablespoon salt

1½ teaspoons paprika

1 teaspoon onion powder

1 teaspoon dry mustard

1½ teaspoons garlic powder

1 teaspoon cayenne pepper

1 teaspoon grated nutmeg

1 teaspoon dried oregano

1 teaspoon ground thyme

¾ teaspoon ground cloves

¼ teaspoon ground allspice

Mix all ingredients and store in an airtight container until ready for use.

About ½ cup

SALMON CROQUETTES

In my family salmon croquettes, or patties, have long been a favorite southern dish, as evidenced by this old recipe from my great-grandmother. Salmon Croquettes II, which follows, is an updated version of this old-time favorite.

¼ cup butter
½ cup all-purpose flour
1 cup heavy cream
1½ teaspoons pepper
½ teaspoon salt
1 cup dry bread crumbs
2 pounds cooked salmon, skinned, deboned, and chilled

2 tablespoons butter
1 medium yellow onion, chopped fine
3 tablespoons all-purpose flour
¼ cup vegetable oil for frying
Parsley sprigs and lemon wedges for garnish

Blend butter and the ½ cup flour together in a bowl. Bring cream to a boil in a small saucepan. Blend in butter and flour mixture. Remove from heat. Add pepper, salt, bread crumbs and salmon. Mix thoroughly and then spoon into a dish to cool. Meanwhile, heat a large, heavy skillet over medium-high heat; add the 2 tablespoons butter and sauté onion until transparent. Add contents of frying pan to the cooled salmon mixture. If the mixture appears too dry, add additional cream. If it appears too soft, add additional bread crumbs. Form into 6 to 8 patties; dust patties with the 3 tablespoons of flour. Cook patties in hot vegetable oil over medium heat until cooked through and golden, approximately 10 minutes on each side. Garnish with parsley and lemon.

6 to 8 servings

SALMON CROQUETTES II

2	16-ounce cans salmon, drained, skinned, and deboned	¾	cup heavy cream
½	cup chopped onion	3	tablespoons all-purpose flour
¼	teaspoon celery salt	¼	cup vegetable oil for frying
¼	teaspoon salt		Parsley sprigs and lemon wedges for garnish
1½	teaspoons pepper		

In a bowl, mix together salmon, onion, and seasonings. Blend in cream. Mix thoroughly; form 6 to 8 patties and dust with flour. Cook patties over medium heat in hot vegetable oil until cooked through and golden, approximately 10 minutes on each side. Garnish with parsley sprigs and lemon.

6 to 8 servings

MOM'S DEVILISH CATFISH STEW

This recipe takes its name from the fact that it is unusually hot. Novices, however, may reduce the amount of pepper called for and still enjoy the unusual flavor of this tasty dish, which actually is a smothered catfish.

3 to 4	pan-ready catfish	¼	cup vegetable oil
	Salt and pepper	1	large onion, sliced thin
¾ to 1	teaspoon red cayenne pepper	2½	cups hot water
	All-purpose flour		

Wash fish, dry, and season to taste with salt, pepper, and cayenne pepper. Dust with flour, shaking off any excess. Heat oil in a large, heavy skillet over medium heat. Oil is sufficiently hot when a drop of water dances on its surface. Add fish to the pan, turning frequently to prevent burning. When fish are done, remove them to a paper towel–covered plate and keep warm. After all fillets have been cooked, add the onion to the pan and sauté until transparent. Add approximately 3 to 4 tablespoons flour to the pan. Cook until the flour browns, then add the water. Reduce heat and cook until gravy begins to thicken. Season to taste with additional salt, pepper, and cayenne pepper. Return fillets to pan and cook an additional 10 to 15 minutes over low heat. Serve with white rice or hominy grits.

3 to 4 servings

"Aside from hunting and horseback riding, nothing rests me more and delights my soul more than to get on some stream near an old-fashioned swimming pool with the root of a tree close by and spend as many hours as I can in fishing with an old-time pole and line."

Booker T. Washington Papers

FRIED CATFISH FILLETS

8 to 10	catfish fillets	3	tablespoons all-purpose flour
	Salt and pepper	2	eggs, well beaten
3	teaspoons seasoned salt	1¼	cups cornmeal
1	teaspoon pepper	¼	cup bacon drippings
½	teaspoon paprika		Enough vegetable shortening
¾	teaspoon onion powder		to deep-fry (2½ to 3 cups)
1¼	teaspoons sugar		

Wash fish and pat dry. Lightly season with salt and pepper and set aside. Combine seasoned salt and next 6 ingredients and mix well. Dip fillets in eggs, then in cornmeal mixture. Place fillets on a wax paper–covered plate and refrigerate at least 1 hour to allow cornmeal coating to set. In a large, heavy frying pan, preferably cast iron, heat bacon drippings and shortening to 370 degrees F. Oil is sufficiently hot when a haze forms above the oil and a drop of water can dance across the surface. Deep-fry fish until golden brown, drain on paper towels, and serve immediately. Excellent with slaw and Hush Puppy Patties.

4 to 5 servings

Waiters at the Twenty-fifth Anniversary Barbecue *(Library of Congress)*

"At first the cooking was done out-of-doors in the old-fashioned primitive style, in pots and skillets placed over a fire. Some of the carpenters' benches that had been used in the construction of the building were utilized for tables."

WASHINGTON,
Up From Slavery

OXTAIL STEW

2 pounds oxtails, disjointed	Pinch of thyme leaves
½ cup all-purpose flour	1 small green bell pepper, chopped
Salt and freshly ground pepper	4 cups beef broth
3 tablespoons vegetable shortening	1 tablespoon vinegar
1 large onion, chopped	1½ cups diced celery
3 garlic cloves, minced	1 cup diced carrots
2 bay leaves	¼ cup all-purpose flour

Season oxtail pieces to taste with salt and pepper and then dredge in the ½ cup of flour. In a large, heavy pot, heat shortening to medium-high, and brown oxtails on all sides. Remove from pan and set aside. Add onion, garlic, bay leaves, thyme, and bell pepper, and sauté until onion is transparent. Next, add beef broth and vinegar. Add additional salt if desired. Cover tightly, simmering over low heat until the meat is tender, 2½ to 3 hours. Add celery and carrots, then simmer an additional 30 minutes. Remove 1 cup of hot broth from the pot, stir into it ½ cup cold water, and slowly blend in the ¼ cup of flour. Mix well until a paste is formed. Return mixture to pot; bring to a boil while stirring constantly. Boil 2 minutes; reduce heat, and continue to cook until the desired consistency is reached. Serve with steamed rice and corn muffins.

4 servings

STEAK AND GRAVY

¼	cup all-purpose flour		4	tablespoons butter
1	teaspoon seasoned salt		2	tablespoons vegetable oil
½	teaspoon paprika		1	large onion, chopped
¾	teaspoon pepper		3	cloves garlic, minced
½	teaspoon garlic powder		2	tablespoons all-purpose flour
1	teaspoon onion powder		2	cups unsalted beef broth
1	beef round steak, about 2 pounds and 1 inch thick		1	cup light cream

Combine flour and next 5 ingredients. Pound mixture into both sides of the meat with a mallet. Sauté meat in 2 tablespoons of the butter and all of the oil over medium heat until brown, about 5 minutes on each side. Remove meat from skillet to a 2-quart baking dish, cover, and keep warm. In the same skillet, sauté onion and garlic over medium heat until onion is transparent; add to meat. Pour over additional butter if necessary. Melt the remaining 2 tablespoons of butter in skillet, blend in the 2 tablespoons flour, stirring constantly and scraping bottom and sides of skillet, until the mixture is smooth and brown. Cook until thick, approximately 3 minutes. Stir in broth and cook, stirring constantly, until bubbly; simmer over low heat an additional 5 minutes. Pour over meat and bake, covered, at 325 degrees F. for 2 hours or until meat is tender. Remove cover and bake an additional 15 to 20 minutes. Add cream, stir, and serve.

4 servings

MY GRANDMOTHER'S MEATLOAF

2 pounds ground chuck or 88 percent to 92 percent lean ground beef
½ pound ground veal
½ pound ground pork (not sausage)
3½ teaspoons Worcestershire sauce
1½ teaspoons garlic powder

¾ teaspoon onion powder
1 teaspoon salt, or to taste
½ teaspoon pepper
1 medium onion, chopped
2 slices white bread, crusts removed
¾ cup light cream
1 egg, lightly beaten

Preheat oven to 375 degrees F. Combine beef, veal, pork, Worcestershire, and seasonings. Add onion. Place bread on top of meat mixture. Slowly pour cream on top of bread to soften it, add egg, and then gently mix into meat. Pat into an ungreased loaf pan and bake for approximately 45 minutes to 1 hour or until done. Serve with Creamy Mashed Potatoes and brown onion gravy, Garden Peas, and rolls.

4 to 6 servings

BRAISED RABBIT

1 rabbit, dressed and cut into serving-size pieces
1¼ cups all-purpose flour
1 teaspoon salt
¾ teaspoon pepper

⅛ teaspoon crushed rosemary
¼ cup bacon drippings or vegetable shortening
½ cup chopped onion

Wash rabbit and pat dry. Combine flour, salt, pepper, and rosemary and use to coat rabbit. Refrigerate seasoned rabbit. In a heavy skillet, heat bacon drippings. Add rabbit to the pan and brown on all sides in the hot drippings. Remove browned rabbit pieces from the pan, and allow to drain on a paper towel–covered plate. Set aside and keep warm. Add onion to the pan and sauté until transparent. Return rabbit to the pan; add sufficient water to cover. Cover the pan with a tight-fitting lid and simmer over low heat until tender, approximately 1½ hours. Adjust seasoning to taste. Serve for breakfast with grits and hot biscuits or for dinner with steamed rice, yams, and hot biscuits.

4 to 6 servings

CHICKEN AND YELLOW RICE

1 teaspoon saffron	½ cup olive oil
2 teaspoons olive oil	1 cup chopped onion
10 to 12 chicken wings (other parts may be substituted)	1½ cups diced green bell pepper
Juice of 1 lime	4 garlic cloves, minced
Salt and pepper	5 cups chicken broth
1 teaspoon ground cumin	2 cups converted rice
1 teaspoon curry powder	1 cup chopped tomatoes
1 teaspoon onion powder	¼ cup pimientos, drained and chopped
1 teaspoon garlic powder	2 bay leaves

Place saffron in a small container with 2 teaspoons of the olive oil and set aside. Wash chicken thoroughly and pat dry. Rub with lime juice. Mix salt, pepper, cumin, curry, and onion and garlic powders together. Season chicken and refrigerate. In a large heavy pot, heat the ½ cup olive oil until fragrant, then brown the chicken 6 to 8 minutes on each side. Remove chicken, add additional oil if necessary, and sauté onion and bell pepper until onion is transparent. Then add minced garlic, being careful not to burn it. Return chicken to the pot, add saffron with oil, broth, rice, tomatoes, pimientos, and bay leaves; bring to a boil. Cook over medium-high heat, uncovered, for 20 minutes. Cover and cook for an additional 20 minutes over medium heat. Season to taste, reduce heat, and allow mixture to simmer 20 to 30 minutes. Add additional water, if necessary; stir in rice, reduce heat to low, cover tightly, and cook until done, approximately 20 minutes more. About 5 minutes before dish is done, remove bay leaves, stir in tomatoes, cover pot, and finish cooking. Excellent with black beans.

6 to 8 servings

"On the good days they had 'white meat' with boiled greens cooked in a big black pot out under the arbor vitae and supplemented with corn bread, molasses, and tea. . . ."

HOLT,
George Washington Carver

SMOTHERED "YARD BIRD"

Chickens had the run of most country yards and soon came to be known as yard bird.

1	2- to 3-pound chicken, cut up	½	cup bacon drippings or
1	cup all-purpose flour		vegetable shortening
¼	teaspoon garlic powder	1	small onion, diced
½	teaspoon onion powder	¼	cup diced red bell pepper
1½	teaspoons seasoned salt	1¾	cups hot water
2	teaspoons pepper	½	cup half and half

Wash chicken. Combine flour and next 4 ingredients and coat chicken; shake off excess. Reserve any leftover seasoned flour, recoat chicken, and refrigerate 1 hour. In a large, heavy frying pan over medium-high heat, melt drippings or shortening. Shortening is sufficiently hot when a haze forms above it and a drop of water can dance across its surface. Reduce heat to medium, add chicken, and fry until the chicken is golden on all sides. Remove chicken to a paper towel–covered platter. Remove all but ¼ cup of the oil from the pan. Add onion and bell pepper; sauté until the onion is transparent. Add ¼ cup of the reserved seasoned flour and brown it until dark golden. Add the hot water and half and half to the pan. Stir until smooth. Then return chicken to pan. Cover tightly and simmer over low heat until tender, approximately 25 to 30 minutes. Serve for breakfast with grits and biscuits or at dinner with rice, biscuits, and yams.

4 to 6 servings

Feeding Geese *(Library of Congress)*

SOUTHERN FRIED CHICKEN AND GRAVY

1	2½- to 3-pound fryer chicken, cut up		⅛	teaspoon garlic powder
1	teaspoon seasoned salt		¼	cup butter
¾	teaspoon pepper		¼	cup vegetable oil
½	cup all-purpose flour		3	tablespoons all-purpose flour
⅛	teaspoon cayenne pepper		2	cups hot chicken broth
¼	teaspoon sweet paprika		¼	cup heavy cream
¼	teaspoon onion powder		½	cup milk
				Salt and black pepper

Preheat oven to 300 degrees F. Wash chicken; lightly season with seasoned salt and pepper; then set aside. Mix ½ cup flour with next 4 ingredients. Flour chicken and shake off excess. Then sauté chicken in butter and oil over medium-low heat, turning frequently until tender and golden, approximately 20 to 30 minutes. Drain chicken on paper towels placed in the bottom of an ovenproof serving dish; keep warm in the oven. Pour off all but ¼ cup of the pan drippings, and stir in the 3 tablespoons of flour. Cook over low heat, stirring constantly, scraping the bottoms and sides until smooth and golden. Add broth to flour mixture, stirring constantly, until bubbly, about 5 minutes. Reduce heat; stir in cream and milk. Simmer uncovered, stirring frequently, for about 20 minutes. Season with salt and black pepper to taste.

4 to 6 servings

"The school's success was in large part due to the tireless effort of the woman who, on August 11, 1885, became Washington's second wife: Olivia Davidson. Born in 1854 to Eliza Davidson, [Olivia and her] family moved to Athens County, Ohio, after the War. Upon graduating from the Albany Enterprise Academy, she, along with her brother, Joseph, and his wife, taught freemen in Hernando, Mississippi. Her brother and sister-in-law were killed by the Klan. Following their deaths, Olivia moved to Memphis and continued teaching. Yellow Fever broke out in Memphis while she was on vacation. Olivia offered her nursing services. However, she had not been immunized, and was ordered to stay away until the epidemic passed. She then enrolled at Hampton where she excelled in her studies and was selected for a two-year scholarship at Framington State Normal School. Three days after arriving in Tuskegee, Booker T., realizing a need for assistance, sent for his friend Olivia Davidson. Working by his side, she assisted with administration, taught, and raised desperately needed funds in Tuskegee. It was Olivia who began the fund-raising efforts in the North. Often in the damp cold she walked house to house all day, every day, soliciting funds for the fledgling school. In the evenings and on Sundays she spoke at churches. She often worked

Olivia Davidson Washington
(Tuskegee University Archives)

to the point of exhaustion. The story is told that on one occasion upon calling upon a Boston lady and sending up her card, she was ushered into a warm parlor. The woman, who was delayed, came downstairs to find an exhausted but warm Olivia curled up on the sofa, asleep.

"In short, Olivia stood shoulder to shoulder with Booker, raised her hands high and helped build a dream called Tuskegee. When not fund-raising in the North, Miss Davidson, in addition to her duties as 'Lady Principal,' taught mathematics, astronomy, and botany. Olivia and five other Tuskegee women organized the first fundraising supper. Every local student was urged to have a relative donate a food item. Going door to door, Olivia solicited donations. One person would agree to donate a cake or pie while another offered to provide chicken. At the appointed hour, the long

Booker T. Washington with Olivia's boys *(Library of Congress)*

table was laden. In addition, girls of the junior class set up a table of candies. One girl moved through the crowd as the 'peanut woman,' while another sold apples." After Fannie's death, Olivia and Booker married. She bore him two children, Booker (Baker) T. Washington, Jr., and Ernest Davidson Washington.

LOUIS R. HARLAN,
Booker T. Washington

"Her life here has been so full of deeds, lessons, and suggestions that she will live on to bless and help the Institution which she founded as long as it is a seat of learning."

BOOKER T. WASHINGTON,
on Olivia Davidson Washington

AT HOME

. . . At home,
the choir prances proudly past
stained glass praises.
Stepping high,—
dancing—
on brightly colored patterns
of early morning light.
Men and women—together
lifting up tireless, unfettered voices.
Griots of shadowy dream/memories,
their bunioned feet vanguard
ancient motherland rhythms.

Intricate, syncopated, vibrating rhythms,
winding, swaying rhythms
Hand clappin'
foot tappin'
shoutin'
rhythms . . .
musky, dark and inviting.

Scarlet robes and billowing sleeves
pirouetting as the spirit moves them.
Their graceful folds evoking fond
memories of countless fund raisers.
Fried chicken dinners, at $1.25 a plate,
served in sweltering heat with collard greens,
and corn bread sponges for sopping pot licker
and creamy lakes of butter.
. . . slabs of sweet cake, jelly cakes, and tater pone

Excerpted from "At Home," by Carolyn Tillery

"One of my earliest recollections is that of my mother cooking chicken late at night and awakening her children for the purpose of feeding them."

WASHINGTON,
Up From Slavery

COUNTRY FRIED CHICKEN

1	2½ - to 3-pound fryer chicken, cut up		2	teaspoons garlic powder
	Buttermilk, sufficient to cover the chicken		1	teaspoon onion powder
			3	teaspoons seasoned salt
	Vegetable shortening		⅛	teaspoon poultry seasoning
1	cup all-purpose flour		1¼	teaspoons ground black pepper

Wash chicken pieces and place in a bowl. Cover with buttermilk and refrigerate a minimum of 2 hours. Melt shortening in a cast-iron frying pan to a depth of about 1 inch. Heat to about 370 degrees F. In a plastic bag, mix together all of the dry ingredients. Remove chicken from bowl. Using additional seasoned salt and pepper, *lightly* season chicken. Place chicken in the bag, one piece at a time. Shake well until thoroughly coated. Dip each piece in the buttermilk and coat with flour once again. (Double-dipping gives the chicken a thick crispy coat.) Shake off excess; place on waxed paper for 15 minutes or until dry. Place chicken, skin side down, in hot shortening. Do not crowd pan. Refrigerate any chicken that does not fit in skillet until first batch is cooked. Brown slowly until golden on all sides. Cover and simmer, turning occasionally, for 35 to 40 minutes or until the juices run clear and chicken is tender. Uncover and cook 5 minutes longer. Repeat with remaining pieces. Test doneness by piercing thickest part of chicken. When done, juice should run clear.

4 to 8 servings

SPICY FRIED CHICKEN

"Finally the great day came and I started for Hampton. . . . When I reached [Richmond] tired, hungry and dirty it was late in the night. . . . 'I was completely out of money.' . . . Knowing nothing better to do, I walked the streets. In doing this I passed many food stands where fried chicken and half moon apple pies were piled high and made to present a most tempting appearance. At that time it seemed to me that I would have promised all that I expected to possess in the future to have gotten hold of one of those chicken legs. . . ."

WASHINGTON,
Up From Slavery

My dear friend Cassandra Bethel, when sharing this recipe, convinced me of the importance of seasoning the meat overnight for the best flavor. The sliced onion puts this recipe "over the top." It is one of my family's favorites.

1	2½- to 3-pound frying chicken, cut up	2	teaspoons seasoned salt
2	teaspoons onion powder	2	large onions, sliced thin
1½	teaspoons garlic powder		Vegetable shortening
½	teaspoon pepper	¼	cup butter
			All-purpose flour

Wash chicken, pat dry, and set aside. Mix together the next 4 ingredients and use to season chicken. In a large nonreactive bowl, thoroughly combine chicken with thinly sliced onions. Cover and refrigerate overnight. In a large, heavy skillet, heat approximately 4 to 5 inches of shortening to approximately 375 degrees F. Add butter to the shortening. (The addition of butter is a trick I learned from my cousin Sweetening. The butter really enhances the flavor.) Discard onions and coat chicken with flour, shaking off the excess, and place in the hot oil. Do not crowd the pan. Cook each side for approximately 15 minutes or until golden. Repeat as necessary. Test doneness by piercing thickest part of the chicken with a fork. When done, juices should run clear.

6 to 8 servings

Concert on White's Hall lawn *(Library of Congress)*

"In Macon county, Alabama, where I live [there is] a kind of church service that is called an 'all-day-meeting.' The ideal season for such a meeting is about the middle of May. The church-house that I have in mind is located abouty 10 miles from town. To get the most out of the 'all-day-meeting' one should make an early start, say eight o'clock. During the drive one drinks in the fresh fragrance of forest and wild flowers. The church building is located near a stream of water, not far from a large cool spring, and in the midst of a grove or primitive forest. Here. . . people begin to come together by nine or ten o'clock in the morning. Some of them walk; most of them drive. A large number come in buggies. . . . All bring baskets of food, for the 'all-day-meeting' is a

kind of Sunday Picnic or festival. Preaching preceded by much singing begins at eleven o'clock. If the building is not large enough, the services are held out under the trees. . . . Sometimes I have seen at these 'all-day-meetings' as many as 3,000 people present. No one goes away hungry. Large baskets, filled with the most tempting spring chicken or fresh pork, fresh vegetables, and all kinds of pies and cakes are opened up."

Booker T. Washington Papers

TASTY FRIED CHICKEN

¼ cup bacon drippings or vegetable shortening	½ teaspoon onion powder
¾ cup all-purpose flour	¾ teaspoon pepper
3 teaspoons seasoned salt	¼ teaspoon chili powder
1 teaspoon garlic powder	1 3- to 3½-pound fryer chicken, cut up

Wash chicken, pat dry, and set aside. In a brown paper bag or a plastic bag, add flour and seasonings; shake well. Place chicken in the bag, a piece at a time, and shake to coat. Shake excess flour from each piece and place it on a plate. Coat the chicken a second time. In a large cast-iron skillet, over medium heat, melt bacon drippings and enough shortening to make 1 inch of cooking oil. When oil is hot, add chicken and fry until brown on all sides. Cover skillet, reduce heat to medium-low, and continue to fry for an additional 25 to 30 minutes, until the chicken is tender and its juices run clear when pierced with a fork. Remove cover from skillet during the last 15 minutes of cooking.

6 to 8 servings

"Aside from the large number of fowls and animals [presently] kept by the school, I keep individually a number of pigs and fowls of the best grades, and in raising these

I take a great deal of pleasure. I think the pig is my favorite animal. Few things are more satisfactory than a high-grade Berkshire or Poland China pig."

WASHINGTON,
Up From Slavery

SMOTHERED PORK CHOPS

4 pork chops	¼ cup bacon drippings or
1 teaspoon seasoned salt	vegetable shortening
¼ teaspoon pepper	1 large onion, sliced
1 teaspoon garlic powder	3 tablespoons all-purpose flour
½ teaspoon onion powder	1 cup water
All-purpose flour	

Wash pork chops and pat dry. Mix seasonings together. Rub on chops (approximately ¼ teaspoon per chop). Reserve remaining seasoning for gravy. Lightly dust chops with flour. Heat drippings in a large, heavy skillet. Add chops and brown each side, approximately 5 to 10 minutes. Remove chops from pan to a warm, paper towel–covered platter. Remove all but ¼ cup drippings from the pan. Add sliced onion to pan and sauté until almost transparent. Add 3 tablespoons flour and remaining seasonings to the pan and brown. The trick is to get the flour as brown as possible without burning it or the onion. Add water and stir. Return chops to pan and add sufficient water to cover. Bring to a quick boil; reduce heat to low; cover and simmer about an hour or until chops are fork tender. Season to taste with additional seasoning mix, if desired.

4 servings

CAJUN RED BEANS AND SAUSAGE

My mother always put her beans on in the morning and tortured the family with their heady fragrance for the remainder of the day until one by one we all crept in the kitchen to sneak a taste. The trick was not to let the lid clatter because, regardless of where she was or what she was doing, she'd yell, "Get out of my pot. You know I don't like folks in my pots."

1	pound dried red kidney beans	¾	teaspoon garlic powder
1	medium onion, chopped	¼	teaspoon ground allspice
1	large green bell pepper, seeded and chopped	¼	teaspoon ground cloves
4 or 5	garlic cloves, minced	½	teaspoon cayenne
½	cup chopped celery	½	teaspoon ground cumin
3	tablespoons bacon drippings	¼	teaspoon gumbo filé
2	quarts water	3	bay leaves
2	teaspoons salt	1	teaspoon Liquid Smoke
1	tablespoon dried thyme, crumbled	1	ham hock, washed
1	teaspoon dried oregano	1	pound link sausage cut into ½-inch-thick slices

A day ahead, rinse and sort beans. Cover with cold water. Soak overnight. In a large pot over medium heat, sauté onion, bell pepper, garlic, and celery in the bacon drippings. Add 2 quarts of water, salt, spices, bay leaves, Liquid Smoke, and the ham hock. Bring to a boil; reduce heat and simmer 1 hour. Drain and rinse beans; then add to pot with enough hot water to cover by 2 inches. Simmer an additional hour, covered, over low heat. Add hot water, as necessary, to keep beans from sticking. (My mother keeps a kettle of hot water on the back burner while she cooks the beans. According to her, adding cold water slows the cooking process and the beans just don't taste as good.) Add the sausage and allow the beans to barely simmer an additional hour uncovered or until very soft, but not mushy. Great served over rice with corn bread on the side.

6 to 8 servings

LOUISIANA GUMBO WITH CREOLE SEASONING

CREOLE SEASONING

1	tablespoon sea salt	1	teaspoon dry mustard
2	teaspoons garlic powder	1	teaspoon ground cumin
2	teaspoons onion powder	1	teaspoon dried oregano
¼	teaspoon dried thyme	1	teaspoon dried rosemary
¼	teaspoon rubbed sage	1	teaspoon dried marjoram
1½	teaspoons cayenne pepper	½	teaspoon crushed bay leaves
1	teaspoon white pepper	¼	teaspoon chili powder
1½	teaspoons black pepper		

Combine ingredients and grind to a fine powder in a food processor or blender. Store in an opaque air-tight container.

Approximately ⅓ cup

GUMBO

This is a time-consuming recipe but very much worth the effort.

2	2-pound chickens cut into 10 pieces each	4	bay leaves
3	tablespoons Creole Seasoning	½	pound andouille sausage or smoked pork sausage, such as kielbasa
3	quarts chicken broth		
1½	cups all-purpose flour Vegetable oil for frying	1	pound large shrimp, peeled and cleaned
2	cups chopped onions	4	crabs, disjointed, with bodies halved, or 1 pound lump crabmeat, picked over
2	cups chopped green bell pepper		
1¼	cups chopped celery		
10	garlic cloves, minced		Cooked rice

Remove visible fat from chicken and rub Creole Seasoning into chicken. Allow seasoned chicken to sit at room temperature for ½ hour. Meanwhile, place broth in a large saucepan and bring to a simmer. While stock is simmering, shake together about ⅔ of the flour and 2 tablespoons of the Creole Seasoning in a plastic or paper bag. Add chicken pieces and shake to coat. Remove chicken from bag and shake off excess flour. Reserve remaining flour for later use. Heat ½ inch of oil to 350 degrees F. in a large, heavy skillet. Fry chicken, skin side down. Do not crowd the pan. Adjust the heat so that the sediment does not burn. Remove chicken as it browns and set aside. Remove all but ¼ cup oil from the pan. Combine reserved flour and additional flour, if necessary, to make ¼ cup. Increase heat under skillet to high. Using a *very* long-handled spoon, gradually stir the flour into the hot oil. Roux is extremely—dangerously—hot. Handle with extreme caution. Stir very rapidly to prevent burning and keep stirring until the roux is a dark red-brown color, bordering on black. Remember that the roux will continue to cook for a few minutes after you remove it from the heat. The trick is to get the roux as dark as possible without burning it. Remove the roux from the heat and immediately stir in the onions, bell pepper, and celery. Continue to stir and carefully spoon roux into the simmering chicken stock. Bring stock to a quick boil. Reduce heat to medium and cook for 30 minutes. Add fried chicken, garlic, bay leaves, and the remaining 1 tablespoon of the Creole Seasoning to the stock. Stir in andouille and reduce heat to low; simmer until chicken is tender, approximately 2 hours. Skim excess fat from top while gumbo is cooking, and stir occasionally to prevent sticking. Just prior to serving, add shrimp and crab. Cook 5 minutes or until the shrimp turn pink and crab turns bright red. Mound steamed rice in individual bowls; serve gumbo over the rice.

10 servings

MRS. VERA C. FOSTER'S FAVORITE SOUTHERN GUMBO

Mrs. Foster said, "Gumbo is one of my favorite dishes. There are various recipes, but the one I like best is southern gumbo. It takes considerable time to prepare, and is not inexpensive. I recommend it for 'special' occasions. P.S. Dr. Foster and I are always pleased to know what the alumni are doing."

1 cup vegetable oil	Tabasco to taste
1 cup all-purpose flour	½ cup catsup
8 celery stalks, chopped	1 large tomato, chopped
3 large onions, chopped	2 tablespoons salt
1 green bell pepper, chopped	4 slices bacon or a large slice of
2 garlic cloves, minced	ham, chopped
About ½ cup chopped fresh parsley, optional	1 or 2 bay leaves
	¼ teaspoon dried thyme
1 pound okra, sliced	¼ teaspoon dried rosemary
2 tablespoons vegetable shortening	Red pepper flakes to taste, optional
2 quarts chicken broth	2 cups chopped cooked chicken
2 quarts water	1 or 2 pounds cooked crabmeat
½ cup Worcestershire sauce	4 pounds boiled shrimp
1 teaspoon molasses or brown sugar	1 pint oysters, optional
	Cooked rice
Lemon juice, optional	

Heat oil in a heavy iron pot over medium heat. Add flour very slowly, stirring constantly with a wooden spoon until the roux is medium brown. This will take from 30 to 40 minutes. Add celery, onion, bell pepper, garlic, and parsley, if using. Cook, covered, over medium heat, an additional 45 minutes to 1 hour, stirring constantly. (You may cut cooking time at this stage, but the gumbo may not be as good.) Fry okra in melted shortening until brown. Add to gumbo and stir well over low heat for a few minutes. At this stage, the gumbo may be cooled, packaged, and frozen or refrigerated for later use. Add chicken broth, water, Worcestershire, molasses, lemon juice, Tabasco, catsup, chopped tomato, salt, bacon or

Women at Tuskegee *(Library of Congress)*

ham, bay leaves, thyme, rosemary, and red pepper flakes, if using. Simmer, covered, 2½ to 3 hours. About 30 minutes before serving, add cooked chicken, crabmeat, and shrimp; simmer, covered, for 30 minutes. Add oysters, if using, during last 10 minutes of simmering. Serve over rice.

4 to 6 servings

This recipe is adapted from *Cooking Across the South*, by Lillian Bertram Marshall (Birmingham: Oxmoor House, 1980), by permission of the publisher.

HAM AND SAUSAGE JAMBALAYA

2	large yellow onions, chopped	½	teaspoon Tabasco
1	large green bell pepper, chopped	2	bay leaves
1	cup chopped celery	½	teaspoon dried thyme, crumbled
4	garlic cloves, minced		
3	tablespoons bacon drippings	¼	teaspoon basil
1	pound smoked sausage or kielbasa, sliced ½ inch thick	¼	teaspoon paprika
		1½	teaspoons cayenne pepper
½	cup tomato sauce	¼	teaspoon whole allspice
4	medium tomatoes, peeled and chopped	4	cups chicken broth
		1½	cups uncooked long-grain rice
¾	pound ham, cut into large cubes		

In a large, heavy pot over medium heat, sauté onions, bell pepper, celery, and garlic in bacon drippings. Add sausage and cook, stirring occasionally, until vegetables are tender, approximately 8 to 10 minutes. Add tomato sauce, tomatoes, ham, Tabasco, and spices. Simmer, uncovered, for 15 minutes. Add chicken broth, bring to a quick boil, and add rice. Cover pot and reduce heat. Simmer 15 minutes. If necessary, add more broth or water, and cook until rice is tender.

6 to 8 servings

JIMMY STINSON'S LOUISIANA CATFISH

2	pounds whole catfish	1	cup blackened catfish seasoning
4	cups Louisiana hot sauce		
2	cups yellow cornmeal	2	tablespoons salt
2	cups all-purpose flour	¼	cup black pepper

Marinate catfish in hot sauce for 2 hours. Meanwhile, mix the meal, flour, and spices together and use it to coat the fish. Heat shortening to approximately 350 degrees F., and fry fish until golden brown. You may have to lower temperature if fish is frying too fast.

4 servings

JOLOF RICE

Named for the Jolof people of Gambia, Africa, Jolof is a stew containing leafy vegetables and, originally, crayfish rather than ham. It is quite similar to red rice.

8 slices bacon	6 cups chicken broth
¼ cup vegetable oil	3 medium tomatoes, coarsely chopped
1½ pounds boneless, skinless chicken breast, cut into 2-inch chunks	¼ cup tomato paste
Salt and pepper	1 teaspoon salt
All-purpose flour	½ teaspoon pepper
½ pound smoked ham, cut into 2-inch chunks	½ teaspoon cayenne pepper
2 large onions, chopped	2 cups uncooked long-grain rice
1 medium green bell pepper, chopped	½ pound medium shrimp, shelled and deveined

In a large, heavy pot, fry bacon until crisp. Remove bacon and set aside on a paper towel–lined plate to drain. Add vegetable oil to the pan. Lightly season chicken with salt and pepper; flour chicken and ham and fry in hot oil. Add onions and green pepper. Cook over medium heat for 5 to 10 minutes. Add chicken broth, tomatoes, tomato paste, and seasonings; stir well. Cover and bring to a boil; reduce heat to medium and simmer for 15 minutes. Add rice; bring to a second boil; reduce heat to low and simmer, covered, an additional 20 to 30 minutes. Add shrimp during last 5 minutes of cooking. Cook until rice is fluffy, shrimp are pink, and chicken tender. Crumble bacon over individual servings just prior to serving.

4 to 6 servings

LOIS'S CRAB ANCHALA

This recipe has been passed down verbally for so long that no one in the family is sure of the correct pronunciation or spelling. However, the taste is always 100 percent correct, and it's one of my favorite meals, especially when served with Cuban bread, as is the tradition in my family.

1½	large onions, chopped		1½	teaspoons garlic powder
1½	cups chopped green or red bell pepper		1½	teaspoons onion powder
7 or 8	garlic cloves, peeled and minced		½	teaspoon celery salt
½	cup olive oil		1½	teaspoons seasoned salt
45	ounces tomato sauce		1	teaspoon ground cumin
1	tablespoon Worcestershire sauce		3	bay leaves
1	teaspoon crushed red pepper		1	cup water
1	teaspoon cayenne pepper		1	dozen cooked blue crabs, disjointed

Sauté onions, bell pepper, and garlic in olive oil. Add tomato sauce, seasonings, bay leaves, and water. Stir sauce until smooth, and allow to simmer, covered, over low heat for approximately 1 hour. Add cooked crab and simmer over very low heat for an additional ½ hour. Serve in a bowl with Cuban bread on the side for dipping in this delicious sauce, or over spaghetti or rice. Try it after or during your next backyard crab boil.

4 to 5 large servings

VARIATION: Substitute 2½ pounds shelled and deveined shrimp for the crab.

6 to 8 servings

CHITTERLINGS

"Chitterlings were often provided to slaves during their Christmas celebration. Booker T. Washington would later recall that hog-killing time came in early December, and for days afterward the slave cabins were supplied with delicious sausage, chitterlings, and side meats. 'It seems to me that there was a certain charm about that Virginia Christmas time, . . . a something which I cannot define.'"

BOOKER T. WASHINGTON,
quoted in "Christmas Days in Old Virginia"

20	pounds chitterlings		2	tablespoons salt
3	large onions, quartered		1	teaspoon cayenne pepper
3	garlic cloves, chopped		2½	teaspoons black pepper
1	bay leaf		2	tablespoons bacon drippings
4	whole Anaheim peppers		4	quarts water

Wash chitterlings in a large pot of warm water. Pull off all but a small amount of the excess fat. Split the chitterlings open; remove all particles and debris. Clean thoroughly. Wash in several changes of water to ensure cleanliness. In a large pot with a tight lid, combine all ingredients and simmer, covered, for 3½ to 4 hours or until tender. When done, cut into 1-inch pieces. Serve hot with white rice, collard greens, potato salad, and corn bread.

6 to 8 servings

"Where's the possum and sweet potatoes?"

PORTIA WASHINGTON PITTMAN,
during a celebration of the eve of her 87th birthday,
paraphrasing Lawrence Dunbar

The night before Portia's 87th birthday "[we] had chicken Mr. Teddie cooked and brought, cornbread and peas Cora brought, pig feet, hog ears, and chitlins I brought—some people call them Kansas City Wranglers—Roy Lee brought the corn whiskey, beer, and gin, and somebody else brought the ice. . . . Vivian and Francis played the piano and sang 'I Like Cake Make No Mistake,' which signaled the cake's arrival."

HILL,
Booker T's Child

PIGS' FEET IN TOMATO SAUCE

4   pigs' feet, split
3½   tablespoons white vinegar
1   tablespoon seasoned salt
2½   teaspoons pepper
½   teaspoon cayenne pepper
2   teaspoons whole allspice
5   whole cloves
1   bay leaf

2   onions, quartered
½   cup chopped green bell pepper
4   garlic cloves, chopped
½   cup sliced celery
4   cups tomato sauce
1   28-ounce can whole tomatoes
2   tablespoons Tabasco

Placed washed pigs' feet in a large pot with sufficient water to cover. Bring to a boil. Add remaining ingredients and reduce heat to low. Cover the pot tightly and simmer slowly for 3 hours or until tender.

4 servings

COUSIN MARGARET'S PIGS' FEET

4 pigs' feet, split	1 pound fresh green beans
1½ quarts kosher pickle juice	5 potatoes, peeled and quartered
2 onions, quartered	

Wash pigs' feet and marinate in the pickle juice overnight. The next day, remove pigs' feet from the pickle juice and rinse. Reserve half of the pickle juice. In a large pot, combine reserved juice and enough water to cover the pigs' feet by 3 inches. Bring to a boil and reduce heat to low. Add onions and simmer, covered, 2 hours; add green beans; cook an additional ½ hour; add potatoes and cook an additional 30 minutes or until potatoes are fork tender.

4 servings

NECK BONES AND RICE

4 pounds pork neck bones	1 medium green bell pepper, seeded and chopped
1 tablespoon seasoned salt	3 garlic cloves, minced
1½ teaspoons onion powder	1 cup uncooked long-grain rice
1 teaspoon garlic powder	½ cup all-purpose flour
1 teaspoon pepper	1 cup water
¼ cup bacon drippings or vegetable shortening	Cooked rice
1 large onion, chopped	

Wash neck bones in warm water, drain, and pat dry. Combine seasonings and use to season neck bones. Heat drippings or shortening in a large, heavy pot; brown neck bones. Remove to a warm platter and then sauté onion, bell pepper, and garlic in the drippings. Return neck bones to the pot. Add water to cover, plus 2½ cups. Bring to a boil over high heat. Reduce heat to medium-low and simmer 1½ to 2 hours, covered, or until tender. Add additional seasoning to taste. Remove 2½ cups of liquid from the pot, and in a separate smaller saucepan bring to a boil. Add rice and return to a boil. Reduce heat and simmer, covered, 15 minutes, until rice is done. Combine flour with water. Stir into pot with neck bones and thicken broth to desired consistency. Stir constantly until smooth. During the last ½ hour of cooking time, uncover pot, increase heat to medium, and allow to cook down for ½ hour. Serve with rice.

4 to 6 servings

BEEF TONGUE

1 fresh beef tongue, about 3 pounds	10 whole black peppercorns
1 small whole onion, studded with 8 cloves	3 bay leaves
1 small onion, chopped	Salt
1 small green bell pepper, seeded and chopped	2 tablespoons cornstarch
	Cooked rice

In a large pot, place the thoroughly washed tongue, whole and chopped onions, bell pepper, peppercorns, bay leaves, and salt to taste. Cover with cold water and bring to a boil. Reduce heat, cover pot, and simmer 2½ to 3 hours. Remove the tongue from the water and allow to cool. When cool, cut gristle and bones from the tongue root. Carefully slit the skin, peel from the tongue, and discard. Slice the tongue thin. Remove 1 cup of broth from the pot, add cornstarch, and mix well. Return to pot; bring to a quick boil, stirring constantly until gravy thickens. Reduce heat to low and return tongue to pot and warm. Serve over white rice.

6 to 8 servings

KIDNEYS AND BACON

2	beef kidneys			All-purpose flour
2	tablespoons vinegar		¼	cup chopped onion
8	strips bacon		½	cup beef broth
	Salt and pepper			

Split the kidneys, crosswise in half and then lengthwise. Trim away, as carefully as possible, all sinew and fat from the kidneys. Place in a small mixing bowl. Add water to cover and the vinegar. Let stand 2 hours. Fry bacon over low heat until done, but not crisp. Remove from pan and set aside. Drain the kidneys and pat dry. Chop into small, bite-size pieces, season with salt and pepper, dredge lightly in flour, and quickly brown in hot bacon drippings remaining in skillet. Remove kidneys. Add onion to drippings remaining in skillet and sauté until transparent. Return bacon and kidneys to skillet; add broth and simmer over low heat, covered, an additional 5 minutes.

4 servings

CARVER'S WILD ONIONS AND GARLIC WITH BACON AND EGGS*

Wild garlic (*Allium canadense*)
Wild onion (*Allium mutabile*)
Wild onion (*Allium vineale*)

All of the above have been relished and found appetizing in early spring when the tops are tender, prepared as follows: Take a few pieces of fat bacon, cut in small pieces, fry until nearly done, and while the grease is very hot stir in the finely cut onion tops [and garlic tops], and let cook until done. Have ready two or three eggs that have been salted and peppered to taste; stir these quickly into the bacon and onions, being careful not to let the eggs get too hard, and serve at once. Some like cheese grated over the eggs before frying.

[1 or 2 servings]

CARVER,
Nature's Garden

"When my father and Mother Sadie returned to the States in May 1920, we moved to Tuskegee Institute. . . . I liked everything I saw in my new home. . . . The family often walked over to the Institute to watch my father review the student body as it marched to Sunday chapel. All the students were in uniform—boys in military dress, and girls in blouses and skirts. My father would accompany Dr. Moton to chapel, but the rest of the family did not usually go. All of us would, however, attend the Sunday band concerts. . . ."

After graduating from West Point in 1936, Davis and his new bride returned to Tuskegee to visit his parents.

"Mother Sadie and my father gave a huge reception for Agatha and me at their home. Among the guests were George Washington Carver. . . . We had a jubilant time, establishing ourselves in the social life of this small community, and for many years it remained our home away from home."

DAVIS,
Autobiography

GIZZARDS AND GRAVY

Seasoned salt
Garlic powder, optional
Pepper to taste
1   cup all-purpose flour
2   pounds chicken gizzards,
     washed
¼   cup drippings or vegetable
     shortening

1   medium onion, chopped
1   small green bell pepper, seeded
     and chopped
2   garlic cloves, chopped
8   cups water
    Cooked white rice

Season and flour gizzards. Retain leftover flour for later use. In a large frying pan, heat drippings over medium heat. Add gizzards and brown on all sides. Add onion, bell pepper, and garlic. When onion becomes transparent, add an additional 2 tablespoons of the reserved flour, stir, and add water. Cover and simmer over medium-low heat for 1½ to 2 hours or until the gizzards are very tender. Add additional seasonings to taste. Serve over rice.

4 to 6 servings

ON THE SIDE

Side dishes are the "something extra" that make a meal memorable. While tastes vary, these dishes can make an individual statement to complement the main course. Personally I would not consider a holiday meal complete without a sweet potato casserole.

I know moon-rise, I know star-rise,
I work in de moonlight, I work in de starlight.

Head got wet wid de mornin' dew,
What yo goin' to do when your lamp burns down?
Mornin' star was a witness too,
What you goin' to do when your lamp burns down?

From an old plantation melody

"Before interested housewives [Dr. Carver] demonstrated the eighteen different ways of cooking cowpeas, all of which they could carry out themselves, to a running accompaniment of words. 'In painting the artist attempts to produce pleasing effects through the proper blending of colors. The cook must blend her food in such a manner as to produce dishes which are attractive. Harmony in food is just as important as harmony in colors.'

"On occasion he would visit the homes of the local farmers. 'With great pride Mr. Henry C. Baker, born a slave, took their guest out of doors to prove how he and his wife benefited by the professor's teaching. . . . They looked at the garden house, where Mrs. Baker exhibited with pride her jars of Hopping John—black-eyed peas and rice already prepared to bring them luck on New Year's Day. For his supper she

brought out meat she had pickled according to his instructions and a jar of jelly sealed
with white of egg.' "

HOLT,
George Washington Carver

BLACK-EYED PEAS À LA CAROLYN

1	pound dried black-eyed peas (the cowpea's kissing cousin)	2	bay leaves
1	large onion, chopped	4	teaspoons seasoned salt
5	garlic cloves, minced	½	teaspoon onion powder
3	tablespoons bacon drippings	¼	teaspoon Liquid Smoke
1	large ham hock or turkey wing	¼	teaspoon ground cumin
		1	pinch crushed red pepper

Place peas in a large colander. Pick over peas, and remove any foreign objects. Rinse under cold water. Place them in a large bowl and add sufficient water to cover by 3 inches. Soak overnight. Drain. In a large pot over medium heat, sauté onion and garlic in bacon drippings. Add washed ham hock and enough water to cover. Bring to a rapid boil, reduce heat, and simmer ham hock, covered, for 1 hour. Add soaked peas, and additional water to cover peas, if necessary. Cover pot and simmer over low heat for ½ hour. Add remaining ingredients and simmer uncovered an additional hour. Add more water if mixture is too thick.

6 to 8 servings

PINTO BEANS

1 pound dried pinto beans	1 teaspoon onion powder
1 large onion, chopped	1 teaspoon garlic powder
¼ cup bacon drippings	¾ teaspoon seasoned salt
1 ham hock or smoked turkey wing, washed	

Place beans in a large colander. Remove any foreign objects and then wash the beans under cold running water. Place the beans in a large bowl and add enough water to cover by 3 inches. Soak beans overnight. In a large pot over medium heat, sauté onion in bacon drippings. Add ham hock and enough water to cover. Bring to a rapid boil, reduce heat, and simmer, covered, for 1 hour. Drain and rinse beans. Add beans with, if required, additional water to cover. Cover and simmer for approximately 1 hour. Add seasonings, stir, and cook, covered, an additional hour or until beans are tender. Remove lid during the last 30 minutes of cooking and allow beans to "cook down" until the broth reaches the desired consistency. Add additional seasonings if desired.

6 to 8 servings

BAKED PINTO BEANS

2 cups dried pinto beans	½ cup molasses
1 medium onion, chopped	2 teaspoons dry mustard
1 cup stewed tomatoes, chopped	1 tablespoon chili powder
2 tablespoons tomato paste	

Pick over beans to remove any foreign objects and soak overnight in enough water to cover by 2 inches. Preheat oven to 250 degrees F. Drain and rinse the beans. Place beans and remaining ingredients in a casserole. Add enough boiling water to cover barely and top the casserole with a tight-fitting lid. Bake 4 to 5 hours or until tender. Add additional water as necessary to keep the beans sufficiently moist. Uncover the casserole and let the beans cook 30 minutes longer without adding additional water.

4 servings

BLACK BEANS

1 pound dried black beans	1 ham bone or 2 ham hocks, washed
¼ cup olive oil	2 teaspoons seasoned salt
1 cup diced onion	3 bay leaves
½ cup diced green bell pepper	1 teaspoon onion powder
1 small jalapeño pepper, chopped	1 teaspoon garlic powder
5 or 6 garlic cloves, minced	¼ teaspoon ground cumin

Place beans in a large colander. Remove any foreign objects, and wash the beans under cold running water. Place the beans in a large bowl and add enough water to cover by 3 inches. In a large pot, heat oil and sauté onion, bell pepper, and jalapeño pepper until onion is transparent. Add garlic. Sauté and stir an additional minute or so. Add water, ham bone or ham hocks, seasoned salt, and bay leaves. Ham should be covered by 2 inches of water. Bring to a boil. Reduce heat to low, add remaining seasonings, and simmer for 1 hour. Add beans and additional water, as necessary, to cover beans. Cover pot and continue to cook on low heat until tender, approximately 2 to 3 hours. Remove lid and allow beans to cook uncovered during the last hour. If beans become too thick, thin with warer. Liquid should have the consistency of a thin to medium gravy. Serve with chicken and yellow rice, corn bread, or Cuban bread.

6 to 8 servings

RED BEANS AND RICE

1 pound dried red kidney beans	2 garlic cloves, minced
1 ham hock, washed	3 bay leaves
¼ cup bacon drippings	1 tablespoon seasoned salt
1½ green bell peppers, chopped	1 teaspoon Liquid Smoke
1 large onion, chopped	1 teaspoon pepper
½ cup minced celery (include a few leaves)	

Place beans in a large colander. Remove any foreign objects. Wash the beans under cold running water. Place the beans in a large bowl and add enough water to cover by 3 inches. Soak overnight. Wash ham hock. Place in a 6-quart pot with enough water to cover. Bring to a boil. Reduce heat to low, cover, and simmer for 1 hour. Add beans and additional water, if necessary, to cover beans by 3 inches. Cover pot and allow beans to simmer over low heat for 45 minutes. Meanwhile, in a large skillet, heat bacon drippings and sauté vegetables. After beans have simmered 45 minutes, add the sautéed vegetables and remaining ingredients to the pot of beans. Simmer uncovered an additional 45 minutes or until the beans are done and liquid has the consistency of a thin to medium gravy. Serve with steamed rice and corn bread.

6 to 8 servings

CREOLE RICE

½ pound fresh small okra, washed and trimmed	1 cup diced smoked ham
3 cups cold water	¼ cup diced Canadian bacon
Juice of 1 lemon	2 large tomatoes, seeded, peeled, and chopped
2½ tablespoons bacon drippings	¼ teaspoon freshly ground pepper
1 large yellow onion, diced	¼ teaspoon ground cumin
2 cloves garlic, minced	5 cups unsalted chicken broth
1 small green bell pepper, seeded and chopped	2 cups raw converted rice

Soak okra for 30 minutes in cold water with lemon juice. The "lemon bath" helps to remove gumminess. In a large saucepan, in hot bacon drippings, sauté onion, garlic, and bell pepper over low heat. Stir in ham and bacon. Continue to cook, stirring, over low heat until onion is transparent. Add tomatoes, spices, and ½ cup of the broth. Cook until thickened, approximately 10 minutes.

Add rice, remaining broth, and drained okra. Stir well and cook, uncovered, over medium heat for 15 or 20 minutes or until most of the water is absorbed and the rice is tender.

4 to 6 servings

RED RICE

5	slices smoked Canadian bacon	3	tablespoons tomato paste
2	medium onions, chopped fine	1¾	cups chicken broth
1	jalapeño pepper, seeded and minced	1	teaspoon salt
		¼	teaspoon pepper
2	medium tomatoes, peeled, seeded, and chopped	⅛	teaspoon cayenne pepper
		2	cups uncooked long-grain rice

In a large saucepan, fry bacon until almost crisp. Remove bacon from the pan, and add onions and jalapeño to the pan; sauté until onions are transparent. Add chopped tomatoes, tomato paste, chicken broth, salt, and peppers. Stir in rice. Cover and cook over medium heat for 20 minutes. Stir in the crumbled bacon and continue to cook for 20 minutes or until rice is tender and all liquid absorbed.

4 to 6 servings

JOHN'S HOME-FRIED POTATOES

In our house everyone cooked, even the men. If extreme youth, age, or some physical handicap prevented you from cooking, then you were expected to watch and pay homage by asking questions and, of course, listening to the stories spun by the cook, whose duty also included passing on tradition through stories. Dad usually made these potatoes on Sunday morning. You couldn't stay in bed while they were cooking.

3	medium baking potatoes	¼	teaspoon seasoned salt
1	large onion, sliced thin	¼	teaspoon garlic powder
3½	tablespoons bacon drippings	¼	teaspoon pepper

Peel potatoes and place in a medium pan with enough cold water to cover them. Bring to a boil over medium heat. Drain the potatoes and refrigerate. When thoroughly chilled, cut the potatoes into thin slices. In a medium cast-iron skillet, sauté onion in bacon drippings. Add potatoes. Add seasonings and periodically shake pan over medium heat until potatoes are golden all over. Serve hot.

4 servings

CREAMY MASHED POTATOES

5	medium russet baking potatoes		2	tablespoons butter
1	cup heavy cream		1	teaspoon salt, or to taste

Bring a large pot of water to a boil. Wash potatoes and place in boiling water. When a second boil is reached, cook 30 to 45 minutes or until fork-tender. Drain water from pot, cover, and allow potatoes to steam an additional 30 seconds, until dry. Remove skins. Add cream, butter, and salt. Using an electric mixer, whip potatoes until smooth. They won't however, be lump-free. Add additional butter, cream, and salt as desired.

6 to 8 servings

"At commencement people from the north were invited down and taken on a Sunday countryside tour. . . . Washington was a showman. Faculty and guests rode in style with a driver for each carriage, and he had relays of horses stationed along the route. This was well planned for the dash, allowing only time to stop briefly at the churches and schools where hundreds were gathered with their eggs and hams and canned goods already out on display. May commencement was, in many respects, similar to the Farmers' Conference, though its emphasis was concentrated more on school activi-

ties. . . . [Although] commencement dramatized education, [it] was not something academic and far away, but close to the parents' own daily life. . . . Many [parents] came from thirty or forty miles away, starting on Tuesday, camping by the wayside, and creaking and rattling in early Wednesday morning, some before daylight. They took possession of the grounds, which became one vast hitching post. . . . As in all times and ages parents yearned to see the results of their sacrifices. They crowded classrooms and shops to touch the strange machinery. . . . On the platform of the chapel they could see a miniature engine to which steam had been piped, or a piece of a brick wall being

Booker T. Washington on platform with President Roosevelt
(Tuskegee University Archives)

laid. . . . Students went through the process of making a loaf of bread, as though it were in slow motion; the dough was mixed, kneaded, and put in the oven, and another loaf was taken out, brown and smelling richly.

". . . At the 1905 Commencement the big news was that the biggest celebration of all would be held next October. President Theodore Roosevelt was planning to visit the school!

"[The] town was agog over the President's contemplated . . . visit. His time would be short and, since he could not possibly cover the grounds, it was decided to put the school on wheels and let it pass in panorama before him on the reviewing stand. Riding the floats were students carrying on the school activities just as they would do in the classroom or at the farm: girls and boys grinning and baling cotton and making butter by old and new methods; girls fashioning brooms and baskets, stuffing mattresses and upholstering furniture, dressing chickens, or sewing uniforms, hats, girdles and collars of 'Alice blue' silk to honor their guest. . . . [T]ailors sitting cross-legged stitch[ed] uniforms.

"Afterward Roosevelt walked to the principal's house through the grounds which, due to Professor Carver's untiring efforts, were beginning to show considerable improvement. The lawns were covered with Bermuda grass, the foliage had grown up before the chapel, and here and there were soft, rich masses of pansies and verbenas. Just before he left, the President telephoned Mrs. Roosevelt to thank her for his birthday message—and how was Quentin?"

HARLAN,
Booker T. Washington

OVEN-ROASTED POTATOES

Great with leftover Sunday pot roast!

2 pounds russet potatoes, quartered or cut into large chunks	1 teaspoon garlic powder
⅓ cup vegetable oil	1½ teaspoons seasoned salt
3 tablespoons dried onion flakes	½ teaspoon paprika
1 tablespoon light brown sugar	1 teaspoon pepper
2½ teaspoons onion powder	2 teaspoons dried rosemary
	Chopped parsley for garnish

Preheat oven to 450 degrees F. Rub prepared potatoes with vegetable oil. In a large plastic bag, combine all dry ingredients. Add oiled potatoes, close bag, and shake until the potatoes are evenly coated. Empty potatoes into shallow, lightly oiled baking or roasting pan. Bake 40 to 50 minutes, stirring occasionally, until potatoes are tender and golden brown. Garnish with chopped parsley.

6 servings

SOUTHERN CORN BREAD DRESSING

3 slices white bread	1 teaspoon dried thyme leaves
Dressing Corn Bread (see next recipe)	½ teaspoon dried basil
1 tablespoon cider vinegar	½ teaspoon marjoram
1 cup milk	2 teaspoons garlic powder
¼ cup bacon drippings or vegetable shortening	2½ teaspoons onion powder
1½ cups chopped onion	1½ teaspoons coarsely ground black pepper
1 cup chopped celery (including some leaves)	2 teaspoons seasoned salt
1¼ cups chopped green bell pepper	1 large egg, lightly beaten
2 teaspoons rubbed sage	3½ cups chicken broth
	4 hard-cooked eggs, chopped

Preheat oven to 350 degrees F. Place sliced bread and Dressing Corn Bread in a large bowl; add vinegar to milk and pour over bread. In a large skillet, melt bacon drippings and sauté onion, celery, and bell pepper until tender, but not mushy. Remove from heat, add remaining seasonings, and spoon into the bowl with the bread mixture. Add remaining ingredients, mix well, and pour into a well-greased casserole pan. Bake at 350 degrees F. for about an hour or as long as necessary to obtain a crusty exterior and soft, but firm, interior.

DRESSING CORN BREAD

1 cup all-purpose flour	1 egg, beaten
1 cup yellow cornmeal	¼ cup chopped green bell
2 tablespoons sugar, optional	pepper
¾ teaspoon seasoned salt	¼ cup chopped onion
1 tablespoon baking powder	¼ cup vegetable oil
1½ cups + 2 tablespoons whole milk	

Preheat oven to 425 degrees F. Mix dry ingredients in a large bowl. Slowly add milk, beaten egg, chopped vegetables, and vegetable oil; mix well; set aside. Lightly coat the bottom of a 6-inch cast-iron skillet with additional vegetable oil and place in the preheated oven for approximately 10 minutes (oil should start to smoke, just slightly). Remove the skillet and add batter. Reduce oven heat to 400 degrees F. and bake for 20 to 25 minutes. May be made up to a day in advance, if kept refrigerated.

8 to 10 servings

BAKED MACARONI AND CHEESE

1½ cups elbow macaroni	¼ teaspoon paprika
2 tablespoons butter	½ teaspoon white pepper
2 tablespoons all-purpose flour	2½ cups grated sharp cheese
¼ cup milk	Salt
1 cup light cream	

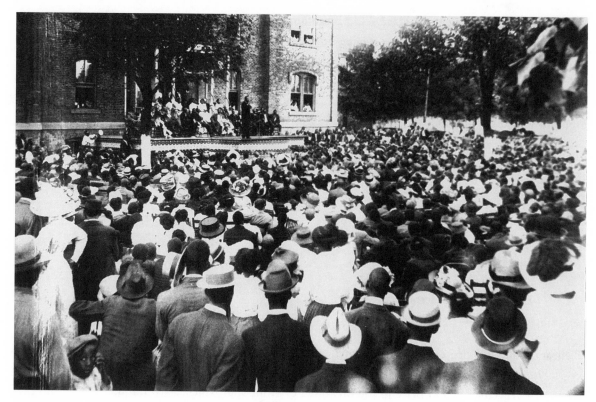

Booker T. Washington addressing students
(Tuskegee University Archives)

Preheat oven to 350 degrees F. Boil macaroni according to package directions; drain and set aside. Meanwhile, melt butter in a medium saucepan over low heat. Blend in flour, stirring constantly. Gradually stir in milk and cream. Cook, stirring constantly, until mixture boils and thickens, about 2 to 3 minutes. Remove from heat and add paprika, pepper, and 2 cups of the cheese; stir until cheese is melted. Gently stir in macaroni and salt to taste. Place in a buttered 1-quart casserole dish. Garnish top with remaining ½ cup of cheese and dot with additional butter. Bake 25 to 30 minutes.

4 to 6 servings

"I was born a slave on a plantation in Franklin County, Virginia . . . in a typical log cabin [where] . . . I lived with my mother, brother, and sister until after the Civil War, when we were all declared free. . . . The cabin was not only our living place, but was also used as the kitchen for the plantation. My mother was the plantation cook. There was no wooden floor in our cabin, the naked earth being used as the floor. In the center of the earthen floor there was a large, deep opening covered with boards, which was used as a place to store sweet potatoes during the winter. An impression of this potato hole is engraved upon my memory, because I recall that during the process of putting the potatoes in or taking them out I would often come into possession of one or two, which I roasted and thoroughly enjoyed."

WASHINGTON,
Up From Slavery

OVEN-ROASTED SWEET POTATOES

6 to 8	medium sweet potatoes	Ground cinnamon
½	cup (1 stick) butter	Grated nutmeg
	Brown sugar	

Preheat oven to 400 degrees F. Wash and dry potatoes. Cut off the small tip from the ends of each potato to allow steam to escape while cooking; lightly grease potatoes with some of the butter. Bake for 40 to 60 minutes. Cut a lengthwise slit in each potato, butter, and season to taste with sugar and spices.

6 to 8 servings

FRIED SWEET POTATOES

7 or 8   sweet potatoes, boiled,
          peeled, and cut crosswise into
          ¼-inch rounds

Salt and pepper
¼   cup bacon drippings
Sugar

Season potatoes with salt and pepper and chill. Fry in bacon drippings and brown on each side. Drain on paper towels, coat each side with sugar, and serve very hot.

4 to 6 servings

DR. CARVER'S CROQUETTES*

Take 2 cupfuls of mashed, boiled, steamed or baked sweet potatoes; add the beaten yolks of two eggs and season to taste; stir over the fire until the mass parts from the sides of the pan. When cold form into small croquettes, roll in the egg and bread crumbs, and fry in hot lard to amber color. Serve on napkins.

SWEET POTATO PUFFERS*

Whip 2 eggs until quite light; two cups of cold mashed [sweet] potatoes: one cup of flour into which one teaspoon of baking powder has been sifted. The potatoes and eggs should be worked together, then the flour and baking powder; roll lightly; cut quickly and fry into deep fat like doughnuts. Some think a little spice improves the flavor.

DR. CARVER'S BAKED SWEET POTATOES*

Scrub with a brush and rinse with water until thoroughly clean. Bake like white potatoes, without breaking the skin. When done break the skin in one place in the form of a cross, forcing the meat partly out, cap with butter and serve. Potatoes from 1 to 1 and ½ inches in diameter, and from 5 to 6 inches long, are the most desirable for baking—the flavor seems to be far superior to the larger kinds, or the round or irregular sort.

DR. CARVER'S SWEET POTATOES BAKED IN ASHES*

In this method the sweetness and piquancy of the potato is brought out in a manner hardly obtainable in any other way. Select the same kind of potatoes as described above for baking; cover them with warm ashes to the depth of 4 inches, upon this place live coals and hot cinders; let bake slowly for at least two hours. Remove the ashes with a soft brush and serve hot with butter.

Booker T. Washington with group *(Library of Congress)*

CANDIED YAMS

8	small sweet potatoes, peeled and quartered		1	teaspoon grated lemon peel
4½	teaspoons fresh lemon juice		⅛	teaspoon grated ginger
¼	cup butter			Pinch ground cinnamon
⅔	cup sugar		½	teaspoon ground nutmeg

Place potatoes in enough boiling water to cover. Add lemon juice and cook until tender. When done, remove potatoes from pot and drain. In the same pot, melt butter over medium heat and add sugar. Stir until sugar melts and begins to bubble, stirring constantly to prevent scorching. When mixture begins to thicken, remove from heat, add lemon peel and spices, and return potatoes to pot, coating with the mixture. Serve immediately or transfer to a buttered glass baking dish and place in a warm oven until ready to serve.

4 to 6 servings

ORANGE-GLAZED YAMS

½   cup butter
1⅓ cups sugar
¼   teaspoon ground cinnamon
1   teaspoon ground nutmeg
⅛   teaspoon ground ginger

¾   teaspoon grated orange peel
½   cup orange juice
3½ pounds yams, cooked, peeled, drained, and cubed

In a medium pot, melt butter and sugar together. Add spices, zest, and orange juice. Bring to a boil, reduce heat, and add potatoes. Gently coat potatoes with glaze. Simmer for approximately 15 to 20 minutes.

6 to 8 servings

SWEET POTATO CASSEROLE

5   cups sweet potatoes, cooked and coarsely mashed
½   cup brown sugar
½   cup granulated sugar
½   cup melted butter
1   teaspoon vanilla extract
1½ cups crushed pineapple, drained

½   teaspoon ground nutmeg
1½ teaspoons ground cinnamon
¼   teaspoon ground allspice
¾   cup pecan halves
¼   cup raisins
1½ cups miniature marshmallows

Mix together potatoes and all remaining ingredients, except the marshmallows. Stir in ½ cup of the marshmallows, and place mixture into a well-greased 13 × 9 × 2 baking dish. Bake at 250 to 300 degrees F. for 30 minutes. Sprinkle the remaining marshmallows on top of the casserole and brown under broiler.

6 to 8 servings

SWEET POTATO AND APPLE BAKE

4 large sweet potatoes, peeled and
   cut crosswise into ¼-inch
   rounds
4 tart green apples, peeled, halved,
   cored, and cut into ¼-inch
   slices
¾ cup honey

¼ cup apple cider
1 teaspoon vanilla extract
1 teaspoon ground cinnamon
¼ teaspoon ground allspice
¼ cup unsalted butter
½ teaspoon salt

Preheat oven to 375 degrees F. In a buttered 13 × 9-inch baking dish, alternate rows of potato and apple slices. Place remaining ingredients in a heavy medium saucepan and bring to a boil over high heat. Immediately pour hot syrup over potatoes and apples. Cover dish tightly with aluminum foil and bake for 1 hour. Reduce temperature to 350 degrees F., uncover casserole, and bake until potatoes and apples are tender and the syrup thickens.

4 to 6 servings

TWICE-BAKED SWEET POTATO DELIGHT

4   small sweet potatoes, unpeeled
2½ tablespoons butter
½   cup golden raisins
2½ tablespoons brown sugar
½   teaspoon ground cinnamon

½ teaspoon ground allspice
1 8-ounce can unsweetened
   pineapple pieces, drained
2 tablespoons chopped pecans

Preheat oven to 400 degrees F. Wash and dry potatoes. Cut off the small tip from the ends of each potato to allow steam to escape while cooking; then lightly butter the outside of each potato. Place potatoes on a baking sheet. Bake 1 hour or until done. Let cool 15 minutes. Cut each potato in half lengthwise; scoop pulp into a bowl, leaving shells intact. Mash pulp and the remaining butter together. Stir in remaining ingredients except pecans. Spoon into potato shells and sprinkle with pecans. Return to oven and bake for 15 minutes longer or until fork-tender.

4 servings

HONEY-GLAZED SWEET POTATOES AND APPLES

8   yams, cooked, peeled, and sliced
    ¼ inch thick
8   tart green apples, peeled, halved,
    cored, and cut into ¼-inch
    slices

1   cup honey
¼   cup apple cider
½   cup unsalted butter
1   teaspoon ground cinnamon

Preheat oven to 375 degrees F. Butter a 13 × 9 × 2-inch glass baking dish. Alternate potato and apple slices in rows in the dish. Combine remaining ingredients and bring to a boil in a medium saucepan. Pour the hot syrup over the potatoes and apples. Bake uncovered for 1 hour.

6 to 8 servings

The class of 1906 (*Library of Congress*)

HOMEMADE CRANBERRY CUPS

4	oranges, halved	1	teaspoon grated orange peel
¼	cup orange juice	1	teaspoon ground allspice
½	cup + 2 tablespoons granulated sugar	1½	teaspoons ground cinnamon
1¼	cups light brown sugar	½	teaspoon ground nutmeg
2	pounds fresh or frozen cranberries, picked over, washed, and stemmed		

Carefully remove pulp from oranges, leaving shells intact. Discard seeds, fibers, and membranes from orange pulp. Combine juice and sugars in a heavy medium saucepan. Bring to a boil over high heat, stirring until sugar dissolves. Add cranberries and orange pulp. Stirring often, cook until the berries begin to pop, about 7 minutes. Remove from heat. Add orange zest and remaining ingredients. Mix well. Cool completely. Cover and chill until cold, about 2 hours. Fill cups just before serving. Cranberry sauce may be made up to 3 days in advance.

Makes 1 quart

CRANBERRY-ORANGE RELISH

2	oranges, quartered and seeded	1	cup granulated sugar
1	pound fresh or frozen cranberries, picked over, washed, and stemmed	1	teaspoon ground cinnamon
		⅛	teaspoon ground cloves
1	cup brown sugar	⅛	teaspoon ground allspice

Peel, seed, and remove fibrous membranes from the oranges. In a food processor, grind oranges and cranberries together to make a fairly course mixture. Mix with sugars and spices and refrigerate. The relish may be prepared and stored in the refrigerator several weeks in advance.

6 to 8 small servings

VEGETABLES

I came to write this cookbook when my husband was reassigned to Air Command and Staff College at Maxwell Air Force Base in Alabama. This allowed me to get reacquainted with the local farmers' markets, with their fresh field peas, crowder peas, fresh collards and turnips. All of these wonderful local vegetables brought back memories of meals I shared at Tuskegee. While researching the history of Tuskegee Institute, I discovered that the first Tuskegee students grew their own vegetables. With food scarce, the first industry taught at the institute was agriculture. A small-scale farm was begun in 1883 on the land on which Huntington Memorial Hall now stands.

"When I can leave my office in time so that I can spend thirty or forty minutes in spading the ground, in planting seeds, in digging about the plants, I feel that I am coming into contact with something that is giving me strength for the many duties and hard places that await me out in the big world. I pity the man or woman who has never learned to enjoy nature and get strength and inspiration out of it."

WASHINGTON,
Up From Slavery

COLLARD GREEN FIELDS FOREVER

Have you ever seen a crop of collards?
It is a vision of magnificence.
Walking along an ordinary road in
Tuskegee one day,
I meandered upon a field
where some industrious hand
had sown the virile plant
as far as the eye could see.
Though the rows were disciplined,
the vigorous jade leaves emanated
an overwhelming energy.
Here was a natural power
sustaining the faded and leaning
houses encircling it.
Spellbound on the field's periphery,
I remembered the Middle Passage,
and pictures of slave quarters at
mealtime whirled.

Collards and cornbread,
communion meal of
daily resurrection.
I ate the survival leaf as I stood at
the field's edge,
soaking its cure through pores
and spirit.

ANEB KGOSITSILE
Reprinted from *Rainrituals*, Detroit: Broadside Press, 1992

Dr. Washington gardening *(Tuskegee University Archives)*

COLLARD GREENS WITH CORNMEAL DUMPLINGS

¼ cup bacon drippings or 4 to 5
   strips of bacon
1 small onion, chopped
1 jalapeño pepper, chopped
1 ham hock or smoked turkey
   wing
2 teaspoons sugar

¼ teaspoon crushed red pepper
3 pounds fresh collard greens,
   cleaned and cut up
2 teaspoons seasoned salt
2 teaspoons garlic powder
¼ teaspoon pepper

In a large pot, heat drippings over medium-high heat, or if using bacon, fry until transparent. Add onion and jalapeño pepper. Fry until onion is soft. Add meat and enough water to cover; bring to a boil. Reduce heat to medium. Cover and simmer 1 hour. Add the remaining ingredients and cook 45 minutes more. Check often and add water as necessary to prevent scorching. Simmer an additional 30 to 45 minutes or until greens are tender.

4 to 6 servings

DUMPLINGS

1 cup cornmeal
¼ cup all-purpose flour
1 teaspoon baking powder
½ teaspoon salt

2 eggs
½ cup milk
1 tablespoon melted bacon
   drippings

Place cornmeal in a large mixing bowl. Sift together flour, baking powder, and salt; mix into cornmeal. Beat eggs and combine with cornmeal mixture. Add milk and drippings. Using a large spoon, drop the batter onto the greens; cover tightly and simmer for 5 to 10 minutes or until done. Serve immediately.

4 to 6 dumplings

TURNIP GREENS

Prepare turnip greens in the same manner as collards, preceding recipe. Peeled, pared, and quartered turnip roots may be placed on top of the turnip greens 20 to 30 minutes into cooking. Because these greens are slightly more bitter, increase sugar to 3½ teaspoons. These greens are excellent mixed with pokeweed, dandelion, or other wild greens.

Students hoeing collards *(Library of Congress)*

POKEWEED*

(Phytolacca decandra)

A plant with which we are all acquainted, and relish when cooked. The leaves and young tender shoots are the choice parts. They should be boiled for two or three minutes in water that has been slightly salted. That water should be drained off and thrown away, then proceed to cook the same as turnip greens. . . .

GREEN BEANS WITH NEW POTATOES

1	small onion, chopped		1	teaspoon seasoned salt
2	tablespoons bacon drippings		½	teaspoon pepper
1	quart water		10 to 12	unpeeled small new potatoes, washed and scrubbed
1	teaspoon brown sugar			
2	ham hocks or 1 ham bone			
3 to 4	pounds green beans, ends and strings removed			

In a medium saucepan, over medium heat, sauté onion in bacon drippings. Add water, brown sugar, and ham hocks. Bring to a boil over high heat. Reduce heat to low and simmer for 1 hour. Add green beans, cover pot, and simmer over low heat, approximately 30 to 40 minutes. Cook a shorter period of time for firmer beans. During last 20 minutes of cooking, add seasoned salt, pepper, and potatoes. Cook until potatoes are tender.

6 to 8 servings

HAM-FLAVORED GREEN BEANS

1	small onion, chopped	2	ham hocks or 1 ham bone
3	tablespoons bacon drippings	2	teaspoons seasoned salt
1	garlic clove, crushed	½	teaspoon garlic powder
2	quarts water	½	teaspoon onion powder
¼	teaspoon Liquid Smoke	3 to 4	pounds green beans, ends and strings removed
1¼	teaspoons brown sugar		

In a medium saucepan, over medium heat, sauté onion in bacon drippings. Add garlic, water, Liquid Smoke, brown sugar, and ham hocks. Bring to a boil over high heat. Reduce heat to low and simmer for 1 hour. Add seasoned salt, garlic and onion powders, and green beans. Cover pot and simmer over low heat, approximately 30 to 40 minutes or until the beans are tender. Cook a shorter period of time for firmer beans.

6 to 8 servings

GLAZED CARROTS

8 to 10	small fresh carrots or 3 cups quick-frozen carrots	¼	cup granulated sugar
	Boiling water to cover	⅛	teaspoon ground ginger
¼	cup light brown sugar	¼	teaspoon grated nutmeg
		3	tablespoons butter

Peel, scrape, and cut carrots into ¼-inch-thick pieces. In a medium skillet, bring water to a boil, add carrots, and cook until tender. Drain carrots and set aside. Mix together sugars and spices and use to coat carrots. In a medium skillet, melt butter. When butter is hot, add carrots and cook over low heat until carrots are glazed and have turned a deep brown color. Stir frequently to prevent burning.

4 to 5 servings

CREAMED PEAS AND PEARL ONIONS

30	small white onions, ½ to 1 inch in diameter, peeled	3	tablespoons cornstarch
2	pounds fresh green peas, or 3 10-ounce packages frozen peas, thawed	2	cups light cream
		1½	teaspoons sugar
5	tablespoons butter	¼	teaspoon salt
		⅛	teaspoon grated nutmeg

Place onions in a medium pot with enough salted water to cover onions by 1 inch. Bring to a boil. Reduce heat to low and simmer, partially covered, for approximately 20 minutes. Reserving the liquid for later use, drain onions and set aside. Cook fresh peas by placing them in 6 to 7 quarts of rapidly boiling water. Cook for 8 to 10 minutes or until tender. Drain the peas and immediately immerse in cold water to stop the cooking process and preserve the bright green color. In a heavy saucepan, melt butter over moderate heat and stir in cornstarch. Remove pan from heat and stir in 2 cups of the reserved onion cooking liquid. Beat mixture 2 or 3 minutes until almost smooth, then add cream. Return the pan to a moderate heat and cook, whisking constantly, until the sauce is thick and smooth. Simmer 3 minutes, then add sugar, salt, and nutmeg. Add peas and onions, then simmer 5 additional minutes or until peas and onions are heated through, and serve immediately.

4 servings

"A good garden is one of the best family physicians. Have a garden, a little place by the house, even if it's only big enough to throw a dipper over it."

HOLT,
George Washington Carver

OKRA WITH CORN AND TOMATOES

3 cups very cold water	1 cup fresh tomatoes, peeled, seeded, and chopped
1 tablespoon fresh lemon juice	Salt and freshly ground pepper to taste
½ cup minced onion	
½ teaspoon minced garlic	
3 tablespoons bacon drippings	
1½ cups sliced okra	
2 cups corn, cut from the cob or frozen corn kernels, thawed and drained	

Combine water and lemon juice. Soak okra in this mixture for 30 minutes to help remove gumminess. In a large cast-iron skillet, sauté onion and garlic in bacon drippings over medium heat. Add okra and continue to sauté over medium heat for approximately 5 minutes, stirring constantly. Add remaining ingredients and continue to cook an additional 10 to 15 minutes. Reduce heat to low, cover, and simmer an additional 5 minutes. Add water as necessary to prevent sticking.

4 to 6 servings

CORN ON THE COB

When buying corn, look for young, tender kernels that are milky inside when split open.

2 teaspoons sugar	Salt and pepper
4 to 6 ears of corn, husked, with silk removed	Butter

Bring a large saucepan of water to a boil; add sugar but do not add salt—it tends to toughen the corn. Place the corn in the boiling water; return to a boil, and cook for 3 to 5 more minutes. The older the corn, the longer the required cooking time. Place corn in a cotton napkin–lined dish. Cover the corn with an additional napkin so that it retains its heat. Serve with butter and salt and pepper to taste.

4 to 6 servings

OVEN-ROASTED FRESH CORN ON THE COB

6 to 8	ears fresh, tender roasting corn	Butter
1½	teaspoons sugar	Salt and pepper

Preheat over to 450 degrees F. Pull down corn husks to remove silk and soak for 10 minutes in enough sugared water to cover. Replace husks and close with a twisting motion or tie closed. Place the ears in the oven and bake 15 to 20 minutes. Remove husks prior to serving, and serve with butter and salt and pepper.

6 to 8 servings

Amelia Platts, a Tuskegee Institute graduate, arrived in Selma in 1929. As a newly hired Cooperative Extension Service Home Demonstration Agent, she taught share-croppers the latest plowing and home canning techniques, in the manner of Carver before her. . . . She also developed a slow cook method which allowed women, working in the fields from sunrise to sunset, to cook while working. A large heated rock was placed in the bottom of a 10-quart metal bucket. Then separate containers of meat, rice, and vegetables were stacked over the hot rock. Finally, the lid was fastened and the entire cooking apparatus packed in wood shavings inside of a larger bucket which could be taken into the field with them. By the middle of the day, their meal was ready.

Following these demonstrations, she and S. W. Boyton, a coworker, would dis-cuss current events, including voter registration and property ownership. Following her marriage to Boyton, she resigned her position. However, they continued to help with the voter registration effort, he with the county agents, she at night in rural churches. When Boyton died in 1963, his last words to Amelia were, "I want you to get everybody registered to vote. . . ." In honoring this wish, Amelia continued to assist in the voter registration effort and was even arrested. Upon her refusal to line up and be arrested, the sheriff grabbed her by the collar and roughly shoved her toward a waiting cruiser. While considering her options, she heard those on line shouting, "Go to jail, Mrs. Boyton; we'll be there with you." By the time of her release, Dr. Martin Luther King began talking of what was to be a historic march to Montgomery.

Despite knowing that she faced serious injury or death, on March 7, 1965, Bloody Sunday, Mrs. [Boyton] was among the first marchers to cross the Edmund Pettus Bridge. Beaten back by troopers with billy clubs and tear gas, Mrs. [Boyton] received blows so severe that her friends pulled her away thinking her dead. The heroic effort of these marchers in the face of brutality took place in full view of the media and virtually guaranteed the passage of the Voting Rights Act of 1965. . . .

Supporters who didn't march, cooked—breads, soups, whatever they could contribute. They were fed coffee and oatmeal in the morning, sandwiches, soups, or fried chicken for the other two meals. During rest stops, meals were served on folding tables.

Montgomery Advertiser,
March 11, 1990

CORN CREOLE

1	medium onion, chopped	1	cup chopped tomatoes
⅓	cup chopped red bell pepper	2½	cups fresh corn cut from the cob or frozen corn kernels, thawed and drained
¼	cup bacon drippings or 4 to 5 slices of bacon fried until crisp		
1	garlic clove, minced	¾	teaspoon salt
2	teaspoons all-purpose flour	½	teaspoon pepper

In a medium saucapan, sauté onion and bell pepper in bacon drippings. Add garlic, being careful not to burn it. Blend in flour and mix until smooth. Add tomatoes, corn, and seasonings. Cook 10 minutes.

4 servings

FRIED CORN

3   tablespoons unsalted butter
2   tablespoons finely chopped
      onion
2½ cups fresh corn cut from the
      cob or frozen corn kernels,
      thawed and drained

1   teaspoon salt
¼   teaspoon pepper
⅛   teaspoon paprika
3   tablespoons heavy cream

In a medium saucepan over medium-high heat, melt butter and sauté onion. Add corn and seasonings. Stir and cook for approximately 10 to 12 minutes or until mixture just begins to brown. Add cream, lower heat, stir, cover, and cook an additional 5 minutes.

4 servings

FRESH CORN PUDDING

12 ears fresh corn or 2 cups frozen
      corn kernels, thawed,
      drained, and finely chopped
1   tablespoon finely chopped
      onion
4   egg yolks, beaten
2   cups light cream

¾   teaspoon salt
¼   teaspoon pepper
½   teaspoon grated nutmeg
4   egg whites, beaten until soft
      peaks begin to form
2   tablespoons butter

Preheat oven to 350 degrees F. With a knife, score the center of each row of kernels. Then, using the back of the knife, press out the pulp, leaving the kernel shells on the cob. Mix together corn, onion, and egg yolks; add cream and spices. Carefully fold in egg whites. Pour into a buttered casserole dish and bake 1 hour or until slightly firm in consistency and golden in color.

6 to 8 servings

CORN FRITTERS

1 cup fresh corn, cut from cob
    and coarsely chopped, or
    frozen corn kernels, thawed
    and drained
2 eggs, well beaten
¼ cup all-purpose flour
2 tablespoons finely ground
    saltine crackers (about 4
    crackers)

½ teaspoon baking powder
1 teaspoon sugar
¼ teaspoon salt
    Pinch of cayenne pepper
    Pinch of grated nutmeg
    Bacon drippings or butter

Mix together corn and eggs; set aside. Sift together dry ingredients and spices; fold into corn batter. Cook by spoonfuls on a hot griddle in bacon drippings or butter.

4 servings

CORN OYSTERS

2¼ cups fresh corn, cut from cob
    and coarsely chopped or
    frozen corn kernels, thawed,
    drained, and chopped
2 eggs, well beaten
¾ teaspoon salt

    Dash paprika
    Dash pepper
¼ cup all-purpose flour
2 tablespoons vegetable
    shortening

In a medium bowl, combine corn, eggs, seasonings, and flour. In a large cast-iron skillet over medium heat, melt shortening. When a haze forms above the shortening and a drop of water can dance across its surface, drop corn batter into the hot oil by heaping spoonfuls. Brown quickly on both sides and serve hot.

6 to 8 servings

FRIED CUCUMBERS

4	cucumbers, pared and cut into ⅛ -inch-thick slices	1	cup dry bread crumbs
	Salt and pepper to taste	¼	cup bacon drippings
2	eggs, well beaten		

Season cucumbers with salt and pepper. Dip slices first in egg and then in bread crumbs. Fry in hot bacon drippings. Brown on both sides, drain, and serve hot.

6 to 8 servings

"In the afternoon the guests traipsed about the campus. They flocked around the stand Professor Carver had set up. There on the spot he was cooking tomatoes, offering them for his audience to taste and eating some himself to prove they were not poisonous."

HOLT,
George Washington Carver

FRIED GREEN TOMATOES

1	cup yellow cornmeal		Pepper to taste
¾	tablespoon all-purpose flour	5	green tomatoes, sliced
1	teaspoon sugar	2 to 3	tablespoons bacon drippings or vegetable shortening
1	teaspoon seasoned salt		
⅛	teaspoon cayenne pepper		

Combine cornmeal, flour, sugar, and seasonings; coat both sides of the tomato slices with the mixture. Place on a wire rack and allow to dry 10 minutes. In a large cast-iron skillet, heat drippings or shortening over medium heat and fry tomatoes in a single layer. Brown each side lightly. Serve immediately.

4 servings

"It was no use teaching the farmers to raise vegetables when their wives did not know what to do with them afterward. On his sorties into the country Professor Carver therefore carried along jars and showed them how to pickle, can, and preserve."

HOLT,
George Washington Carver

GREEN TOMATO CHOW CHOW

1	peck (8 quarts) green tomatoes, sliced		1	tablespoon table salt
12	large white onions, thinly sliced		20	small red hot peppers, sliced thin
1	cup pickling salt		2	tablespoons + 2 teaspoons whole cloves
3	quarts cider vinegar		2	tablespoons + 2 teaspoons whole allspice
10	green bell peppers, thinly sliced		1	tablespoon + 1 teaspoon celery seed
8	red bell peppers, diced		2	3-inch cinnamon sticks
6	garlic cloves, minced		3 or 4	bay leaves
8	cups brown sugar			
2	tablespoons dry mustard			

Sprinkle the sliced tomatoes and onions with pickling salt. Refrigerate for 12 hours or overnight. Rinse under cold running water and drain. In a large saucepan, bring vinegar to a boil. Add green peppers, red peppers, garlic, brown sugar, dry mustard, and table salt. Add tomatoes, hot peppers, cloves, allspice, celery seed, cinnamon sticks, and bay leaves. Reduce heat, simmering approximately 1 hour or until the tomatoes are transparent. Stir frequently. When done, place in sterile, hot, airtight jars. Seal according to manufacturer's directions.

Makes about 6 quarts

Pickled Beets and Onions

1	16-ounce can (2 cups) sliced beets, with juice		1	teaspoon sugar
2	tablespoons vegetable oil		½	teaspoon salt
¼	cup cider vinegar		1	onion, sliced thin
3	whole cloves			

Drain beet juice into a serving dish. Blend in oil, vinegar, cloves, sugar, and salt. Finally, add beets and onion; refrigerate 1 hour.

4 to 6 servings

Red Beets and Boiled Eggs

1	16-ounce can (2 cups) sliced beets, with juice		½	teaspoon salt
½	cup cider vinegar		7	hard-cooked eggs, peeled
1½	teaspoons sugar			Bibb lettuce leaves

Open can of beets and drain juice into a medium bowl. Add vinegar, sugar, and salt. Place eggs in the bowl with the beet juice. Roll the eggs in the juice until they are completely colored. Return the beets to the juice and refrigerate overnight. Turn the eggs occasionally to ensure even color. The next day, serve the beets on a bed of Bibb lettuce and garnish with the whole hard-cooked eggs. This dish is especially attractive served on Easter Day in a ceramic basket or other basketlike container.

4 to 6 servings

"About a year after the school was started, construction of Porter Hall began. The third floor was used as a girls' dormitory (at that time, the boys boarded with families in town, for about 6 or 7 dollars a month), and the first and second floors were used as classrooms and offices. It also housed a dining room, laundry, and kitchen. The fare was plain. A

long table with an oilcloth cover, cheap iron knives and forks, and the cheapest crockery cups and dishes were the proud possessions of this pioneer group of students and teachers. Although Porter Hall was dedicated in the spring of 1881, the students kept coming. Another building was needed. Washington decided that the second building, Alabama Hall, should be built of brick. 'A half mile out beyond Porter Hall they began digging clay for brick. No one knew how to construct a kiln, and one after another failed until Washington pawned his watch to secure funds for a final effort.' No amount of work and sacrifice was too much to make this dream come true. This gift of hands teaching hands pride and self reliance—This experiment could not and WOULD NOT fail."

HOLT,
George Washington Carver

Students laying brick *(Library of Congress)*

BREADS

Bread has been called the staff of life, and the time-consuming yet satisfying tasks of kneading dough and baking bread have changed little since days long ago when the first brick ovens were built at Tuskegee in the 1880s. Think of the recipes in this section as a way of reaching back to the delicious traditions that sustained past generations.

The Institute grounds around the beginning of the century
(Library of Congress)

"Wednesday and Sundays [we] were supposed to have light bread, but wood was used
for heating and for firing the kilns, which came first; there was not always enough left
to cook the bread thoroughly and the center was often raw dough. Later [we] made a

long oven of clay and at night set in it lighted Aladdin lamps a yard apart. This did a better job; in the morning Mr. Branum would withdraw more palatable food."

HOLT,
George Washington Carver

"At the close of the sixteenth year parents came from thirty and forty miles away to attend a commencement. 'A place in the bottom land was set aside where they could sit and eat.' With pride, the school provided the five hundred loaves of bread, the ox, and hundreds of gallons of coffee required to feed them."

HOLT,
George Washington Carver

CHURCH SOCIAL YEAST BISCUITS

These blue-ribbon diet-busters are, without exception, absolutely delicious!

1 package active dry yeast	¼ cup sugar
½ cup warm water (110 to 115 degrees F.)	3 cups all-purpose flour
½ cup butter	1 teaspoon salt
1 egg	½ cup boiling water

Dissolve yeast in warm water. Beat butter, egg, and sugar; add dissolved yeast and stir. Add flour, salt, and boiling water; mix well. Refrigerate dough overnight or until well chilled. Preheat oven to 350 degrees F. Roll out dough to ¾-inch thickness and cut into biscuits. Reroll scraps and cut again until all dough is used. Let biscuits rise 1½ to 2 hours, and bake until golden brown, approximately 12 to 15 minutes.

12 to 18 biscuits

BUTTER ROLLS

1	cup milk	½	cup sugar
1	cake compressed yeast	1	tablespoon honey
¼	cup butter	3	eggs
½	teaspoon salt	5½	cups enriched flour, sifted
¼	cup solid vegetable shortening	½	cup melted butter

Preheat oven to 425 degrees F. In a medium saucepan, heat milk until small bubbles form on side of pan, and cool to lukewarm. Add yeast to milk and stir until dissolved. In a large bowl, cream butter, salt, and shortening; gradually add sugar and honey. Add eggs, one at a time, and beat well. Gradually add flour, alternating with milk mixture, mixing well after each addition. Beat for 2 or 3 minutes after final addition. Place in a greased bowl, cover with a tea towel, and allow to rise in a warm place 1 hour or until double in bulk. Cover tightly with plastic wrap and refrigerate several hours or until chilled. Turn out onto a floured board, roll out to a thickness of ½ inch, and cut out with floured biscuit cutter. Reroll scraps and cut again until all dough is used. Place in a greased pan, brush with melted butter, and let rise until double in size, about 35 minutes. Bake 10 to 15 minutes or until golden.

2 dozen rolls

BUTTERMILK ROLLS

1	teaspoon sugar	1	teaspoon baking soda
½	cup warm water (110 to 115 degrees F.)	2	tablespoons solid vegetable shortening
3	packages active dry yeast	2	cups warm buttermilk
5	cups self-rising flour	1	cup butter
¼	cup sugar		

Add 1 teaspoon of the sugar to warm water and dissolve yeast in the mixture; set aside. In a large mixing bowl, combine flour, the ¼ cup sugar, and baking soda. Cut in shortening until the mixture resembles coarse meal. Stir in yeast mixture and buttermilk; mix well. Turn out onto a lightly floured surface; knead lightly a few times. Roll out to a ½-inch thickness. Cut with a floured biscuit cutter. Reroll scraps and cut again until all dough is used. Melt butter, dip biscuits into melted butter, and arrange them on a cookie sheet. Cover and let rise approximately 1 hour. Bake at 400 degrees F. for 10 minutes or until golden.

2 dozen rolls

POTATO ROLLS

1	large baking potato, cooked and peeled	1	teaspoon salt
1	package active dry yeast	¾	cup solid vegetable shortening
1	cup warm water (110 to 115 degrees F.)	1	cup half and half, scalded
1	cup sugar	2	eggs, well beaten
		5	cups flour, approximately
		1	cup melted butter

In a large bowl, mash potato (there should be about 1 cup) and set aside. In a separate bowl, combine yeast with warm water and set aside to proof. Add sugar, salt, and shortening to bowl with potato. Pour scalded half and half over the mixture. Add yeast and remaining ingredients and mix well. Cover with a tea towel and allow to rise overnight, or at least 8 hours. Roll dough out to ½-inch thickness, and cut into circles with a floured biscuit cutter. Reroll scraps and cut again until all dough is used. Dip each roll in melted butter, fold in half, and place in a lightly greased baking pan, approximately ½ inch apart. Allow to rise for an hour before baking at 350 degrees F. for 20 minutes.

2 dozen rolls

SALLY LUNN

1	cup light cream	4	cups all-purpose flour, sifted
1	package active dry yeast	1	teaspoon salt
½	cup softened butter	½	teaspoon ground mace
⅓	cup granulated sugar		Confectioners' sugar
3	eggs, well beaten		

Heat cream until small bubbles form on side of pan, and cool to lukewarm. Sprinkle yeast over the cream, and stir until yeast dissolves. Cream together butter and sugar until light and fluffy. Add beaten eggs, beating well. In a separate bowl, sift flour, salt, and mace together. Beat flour mixture and light cream alternately into the creamed butter. Cover dough with a tea towel, and set in a warm place until double in size, about 1½ to 2 hours. Punch down, and pour into a greased 10-inch tube or angel cake pan. Preheat oven to 350 degrees F. Let dough rise again until double in size, and then bake for 45 to 50 minutes. Remove from pan, cool on a wire rack, and sprinkle lightly with confectioners' sugar.

10 to 12 servings

DR. CARVER'S SWEET POTATO BISCUITS*

1	cup boiled and finely mashed sweet potatoes	1	teaspoon salt
2	well-beaten eggs	2	scant tablespoons melted butter or lard
2	cups [all-purpose] flour	1	tablespoon sugar (if desired)
2	teaspoons baking powder	2	cups milk

Mix together all the dry ingredients. Stir beaten eggs and potatoes into the milk. [Add dry ingredients to the milk mixture.] If the mixture is too soft, add sufficient flour to make a soft dough. Roll out lightly, cut with a biscuit cutter, and bake in a hot oven for about 15 minutes.

[1 dozen biscuits]

CARVER,
Sweet Potatoes

SWEET POTATO BISCUITS

2   cups cooked and mashed sweet
     potatoes
¼   cup softened butter
½   cup + 2 tablespoons light cream
1   tablespoon honey or pure maple
     syrup

1¾   cups all-purpose flour
2   teaspoons baking powder
½   teaspoon salt
⅛   teaspoon grated nutmeg

Preheat oven to 450 degrees F. Mix together potatoes and butter. Add cream and honey. In a separate bowl, sift together remaining ingredients. Combine the sweet potato mixture and flour mixture to form a soft dough. Turn out on a floured board and knead very lightly 5 times, or until the outside looks smooth. Roll out to a ½-inch thickness, and cut biscuits. Reroll scraps and cut again until all dough is used. Place biscuits ½ inch apart on an ungreased baking sheet. Bake 20 minutes or until golden. Serve warm.

2 dozen biscuits

PEANUT BUTTER BISCUITS

2   cups all-purpose flour, sifted
2   teaspoons baking powder

½   cup creamy peanut butter
¾   cup milk

Preheat oven to 450 degrees F. In a large mixing bowl, sift together flour and baking powder; cut in peanut butter until mixture resembles coarse meal. Gradually add milk until a soft dough is formed. On a lightly floured board, gently knead 8 or 10 times, turning dough over 2 or 3 times during this process. With a floured rolling pin, roll out the dough to a ½-inch thickness, and cut with a floured biscuit cutter. Reroll scraps and cut again until all dough is used. Place the biscuits close together on an ungreased cookie sheet, and bake 10 to 15 minutes or until brown.

2 dozen biscuits

BAKING POWDER BISCUITS

2½	cups all-purpose flour, sifted		½	teaspoon cream of tartar
1	tablespoon baking powder		½	cup softened butter
2	teaspoons sugar		¾	cup milk
½	teaspoon salt			

Measure flour and sift all the dry ingredients together. Cut in butter until the mixture resembles coarse meal. Form a wet dough with the milk. Knead 8 or 10 times. With a floured hand, pat dough out to a ½-inch thickness. Cut out biscuits with a floured biscuit cutter. Pat out scraps and cut again until all dough is used, and refrigerate biscuits for 1 hour. Preheat oven to 450 degrees F. Bake for 12 or 15 minutes or until golden.

2 dozen biscuits

DROP BISCUITS

2	cups all-purpose flour, sifted		1	tablespoon sugar
3½	teaspoons baking powder		3	tablespoons butter
1	teaspoon salt		1¼	cups milk

Preheat oven to 450 degrees F. Sift dry ingredients into a mixing bowl. Cut in the butter; add milk and mix into a dough. Drop by spoonfuls onto a lightly buttered baking sheet. Bake until light brown, approximately 12 to 15 minutes.

2 dozen biscuits

BUTTERMILK BISCUITS

2	cups all-purpose flour	½	teaspoon salt
2	teaspoons baking powder	¼	cup vegetable shortening
½	teaspoon baking soda	¾	cup buttermilk

Preheat oven to 450 degrees F. In a large bowl, combine the first 4 ingredients. Using a fork or pastry blender, cut in shortening until the mixture resembles coarse cornmeal. Blend in the buttermilk until a soft dough is formed. Turn out onto a lightly floured surface, and knead lightly 7 or 8 times. Roll to ½-inch thickness, and cut out with a floured biscuit cutter. Reroll scraps and cut until all dough is used. Place biscuits on an ungreased cookie sheet, about 1 inch apart, and bake until golden, approximately 15 minutes.

Makes about a dozen to a dozen and a half biscuits, depending on the size cutter used

QUICK AND EASY BISCUITS

Thanks, Mrs. Burke!

2	cups all-purpose flour	1	tablespoon baking powder
1	teaspoon salt	⅔	cup milk
1¼	teaspoons confectioners' sugar	⅓	cup vegetable oil

Preheat oven to 450 degrees F. Combine dry ingredients and set aside. Combine milk and oil; add to dry ingredients and gently mix until just blended and the mixture forms a wet dough. Place dough on a lightly floured surface and gently knead 8 or 10 times. Pat dough out to a ½-inch thickness. Cut out biscuits with a floured biscuit cutter. Pat out scraps and cut until all dough is used. Arrange on an ungreased baking sheet, and bake for 12 to 15 minutes, until golden. Makes a wonderfully light and fluffy biscuit.

2 dozen biscuits

PEPPERED BUTTERMILK BISCUITS

3¾ cups unbleached all-purpose flour	6 tablespoons unsalted butter
2 tablespoons baking powder	⅓ cup solid vegetable shortening
2 teaspoons freshly ground pepper	1 cup chilled milk
1¼ teaspoons salt	¼ cup chilled light cream
	⅓ cup chilled buttermilk

Preheat oven to 450 degrees F. In a large bowl, combine the first 4 ingredients. Cut butter and shortening into small pieces and add to the flour; rub into flour with fingertips until coarse crumbs form. Mix in milk, cream, and buttermilk to form a soft dough. Turn dough out onto a floured surface and gently knead until combined, about half a minute. With a rolling pin, roll dough to a thickness of ½ inch. Cut out biscuits with a biscuit cutter. Roll out scraps and cut again until all dough is used. Arrange on an ungreased baking sheet, and bake until golden, about 15 minutes.

2 dozen biscuits

VANILLA CREAM BISCUITS

2 cups all-purpose flour, sifted	1 cup heavy cream
3 teaspoons baking powder	1 teaspoon vanilla extract
½ teaspoon salt	

Preheat oven to 425 degrees F. In a large bowl, sift together dry ingredients. In another bowl, whip cream until sufficiently stiff to hold a peak. Combine cream, vanilla extract, and dry ingredients to form a soft dough. Place on a lightly floured board and roll to a thickness of ½ inch. Cut with a small biscuit cutter. Reroll scraps until all dough is used. Arrange on a lightly greased baking sheet, and bake for 10 to 12 minutes, until golden.

2 dozen biscuits

J.R.'s SKILLET CORN BREAD

My own family follows the tradition of everyone in the house cooking. My husband, J.R., is a passably good cook but an excellent baker. His corn bread is a family favorite. At family gatherings he is always enlisted to bake the bread. His secret ingredient: a pinch of nutmeg.

1	cup all-purpose flour		Pinch of ground nutmeg
½	cup yellow cornmeal	1	cup whole milk
¼	cup sugar, optional	1	egg, beaten
¾	teaspoon salt, optional	¼	cup vegetable oil
3	teaspoons baking powder		

Preheat oven to 425 degrees F. Mix dry ingredients in a large bowl. Slowly add milk, beaten egg, and vegetable oil, and mix well; set aside. Coat a 10-inch cast-iron skillet with additional vegetable oil, and place in preheated oven for approximately 10 to 15 minutes (oil should start to smoke). Remove the skillet and pour in batter. Reduce oven heat to 400 degrees F. and bake for 20 to 25 minutes. Remove bread from oven and brown under a broiler. Turn out onto an ovenproof plate and serve hot with melted butter.

6 to 8 servings

WHOLE WHEAT CORN BREAD

I discovered this recipe quite by accident, and it quickly became a family favorite. This corn bread is excellent with fresh vegetable beef soup because of its heartier texture.

¼	cup vegetable shortening	1	tablespoon baking powder
1	cup yellow cornmeal	½	teaspoon salt
1	cup whole wheat flour	1½	cups milk
2	tablespoons sugar	1	egg, beaten

Heat shortening in a 10-inch cast-iron skillet for 10 to 15 minutes. While skillet is heating, combine dry ingredients in a mixing bowl. Add milk and egg; mix until blended. Remove skillet from oven and tilt to coat evenly with the melted shortening. Pour the melted shortening into the cornmeal mixture, and stir well. Pour back into the hot skillet, and bake for 20 to 25 minutes or until a wooden pick inserted into the center comes out clean.

6 to 8 servings

SPOON BREAD

2	cups water	1	tablespoon sugar
1	cup cornmeal	½	teaspoon salt
3	eggs, beaten	1	cup heavy cream
2	teaspoons baking powder	2	tablespoons butter, melted

Preheat oven to 350 degrees F. In a medium saucepan, mix water and cornmeal. Bring to a boil and cook 5 minutes. Cool to lukewarm. Add eggs and remaining ingredients. Beat thoroughly; pour into a well-greased pan and bake 30 to 40 minutes or until puffed and golden. Serve as an alternative to bread.

6 to 8 servings

JOHNNY OR JOURNEY CAKES

In my family this bread was called hot-water corn bread. Some people substitute 1 cup milk for 1 cup of the water. I think the old way is best, especially with a "mess of greens."

1	cup cornmeal	1½	cups boiling water
1	teaspoon salt	3	tablespoons vegetable
1	teaspoon sugar		shortening

Heat a cast-iron skillet over medium heat, melt 3 tablespoons of shortening in the pan. While skillet is heating, in a medium bowl, combine cornmeal, salt, sugar, and boiling water. Stir until smooth and then drop in batter by heaping spoonfuls into the hot skillet. Fry on each side for approximately 3 to 5 minutes. For a thinner cake, thin batter with ¼ to ½ cup milk.

10 to 12 small rounds

CRACKLING BREAD

3	ounces salt pork, chopped	¾	cup all-purpose flour
1	cup stone ground yellow cornmeal	1	cup milk
2	teaspoons baking powder	2	eggs
1	teaspoon salt	3	tablespoons bacon drippings or vegetable oil
½	teaspoon ground nutmeg		

Preheat oven to 425 degrees F. To make cracklings, in a saucepan, cover salt pork with water and bring to a boil. Boil 2 minutes, drain, rinse, and cover with water again. Bring to a second boil. Allow water to boil away. Reduce heat and fry until crisp. Remove cracklings to a paper-towel-lined plate to drain. Grease a 10-inch cast-iron skillet and place in oven. While skillet is heating, combine cornmeal and remaining ingredients in a medium bowl. Mix well. Gently stir cracklings into the batter. Remove pan from the oven. Pour batter into pan and bake 35 to 40 minutes, until golden.

6 to 8 servings

CORN STICKS

¾	cup yellow cornmeal	3	tablespoons vegetable oil
½	cup all-purpose flour	1	large egg, beaten
4	teaspoons maple syrup	1½	teaspoons baking powder
¾	teaspoon salt	¾	cup milk

Preheat oven to 450 degrees F. Generously brush a cast-iron corn stick molds with vegetable oil. Place molds in oven and preheat 15 minutes. Combine all ingredients in a large bowl and beat well with a wooden spoon. Fill molds. Bake until golden brown, about 10 to 15 minutes. Serve hot.

12 corn sticks

HUSH PUPPY PATTIES

3	tablespoons chopped onion	½	teaspoon onion powder
1	cup cornmeal	¼	teaspoon garlic powder
½	cup all-purpose flour	⅛	teaspoon cayenne pepper
1	teaspoon baking powder	1	egg
½	teaspoon salt	¾	cup milk
2	teaspoons sugar		Vegetable oil for frying

Combine onion and dry ingredients, and set aside. Beat together egg and milk, and then combine with dry ingredients. Heat 2 inches of vegetable oil in a large skillet to 370 degrees F. Drop batter by heaping spoonfuls into hot oil and fry until golden.

12 to 15 servings

CORN GEMS

1	cup milk	½	teaspoon salt
1	cup light cream	2	cups yellow cornmeal
3	egg yolks, well beaten	1	teaspoon cream of tartar
1	cup all-purpose flour	½	teaspoon baking powder
1	tablespoon butter, melted	3	egg whites, well beaten

Preheat oven to 400 degrees F. Bring milk and cream to a boil; cool to lukewarm. Blend in egg yolks. Add flour and blend. Add the melted butter and salt, and beat well. Mix in the cornmeal, cream of tartar, and baking powder. Stir in egg whites until thoroughly mixed. Fill 12 greased gem or muffin tins two-thirds full and bake for 25 minutes.

12 servings

HONEY CORN MUFFINS WITH RASPBERRY BUTTER

MUFFINS

1	cup cornmeal	1	cup heavy cream
½	cup all-purpose flour	3	tablespoons honey
3	teaspoons baking powder	3	tablespoons water
⅛	teaspoon grated nutmeg	2	eggs, well beaten
¾	teaspoon salt	3	tablespoons melted butter

Preheat oven to 375 degrees F. Mix together dry ingredients. Add cream, and remaining ingredients. Mix well and spoon into paper-lined muffin cups. Bake 20 minutes or until golden.

12 servings

RASPBERRY BUTTER

1 cup fresh raspberries	2 tablespoons confectioners' sugar
2 tablespoons water	2 teaspoons raspberry liquor
1½ tablespoons granulated sugar	
½ cup unsalted butter, room temperature	

Boil raspberries, water, and granulated sugar over medium heat for about 5 minutes. Strain the mixture into a small bowl. Place raspberry mixture, butter, confectioners' sugar, and raspberry liquor into a blender or food processor. Blend until smooth. Transfer to a small serving container, cover, and chill for 1 hour prior to serving with corn muffins.

About 1½ cups

DR. CARVER'S SWEET POTATO MUFFINS*

1 sweet potato, weighing about ¾ pound	2 well-beaten eggs
1 heaping tablespoon butter	½ cup milk
Pinch of salt	1 teaspoon baking powder
	2 cups flour

Boil sweet potato until thoroughly done. Mash very fine and pass through a colander to remove any lumps, add butter, a little salt, and whip well. Now add eggs and ½ cup of milk, sift in baking powder and enough flour to make a soft batter. Bake in muffin or gem pans in a 400 degree oven for about 30 minutes.

[Approximately 12 muffins]

CARVER,
Sweet Potatoes

HOE CAKES

It is said these cakes were so named because they were cooked by slaves over open fires on the flat side of a field hoe.

5	tablespoons bacon drippings or vegetable shortening for frying	1	teaspoon salt
2	tablespoons all-purpose flour	½ to ¾	cup milk
2	cups cornmeal	½	teaspoon baking soda
		1	egg

In a medium bowl, mix 1 tablespoon of drippings with remaining ingredients. Preheat a cast-iron skillet over medium heat. Add remaining 4 tablespoons of the bacon drippings or shortening to the skillet. Drop round cakes of the cornmeal batter, approximately 1 or 1½ inches thick, into the skillet. Fry 1 or 2 minutes or until golden on each side. Drain on paper towels and serve hot.

8 to 12 servings

SWEET POTATO BREAD

5¼	cups all-purpose flour	6	eggs
3	teaspoons baking soda	1½	cups pineapple juice
3	teaspoons ground cinnamon	3	cups cooked, mashed sweet potatoes
2	teaspoons ground nutmeg	½	cup heavy cream
1	teaspoon ground allspice	2	teaspoons vanilla extract
2¼	teaspoons salt	½	cup golden raisins
2	cups brown sugar	¾	cup pecan halves
2	cups white sugar		
1½	cups vegetable oil		

Preheat oven to 325 degrees F. Grease and flour three 9¼ × 5¼ × 2¾-inch loaf pans; set aside. Combine flour and next 5 ingredients. Combine the sugars, oil, eggs, pineapple juice, and sweet potatoes. Add to dry ingredients, and beat together. Stir in cream, vanilla extract, raisins, and nuts. Pour into prepared loaf pans and bake for 75 to 90 minutes or until toothpick comes out clean when inserted in the middle of the bread.

3 large loaves

Principal Washington's home *(Library of Congress)*

DR. CARVER'S OATMEAL PEANUT BREAD*

2   cups liquid yeast
2   cups rolled oats
2   teaspoons sugar
1   teaspoon salt

1   tablespoon butter
     White flour
1   cup chopped peanuts

[Mix together first 5 ingredients, and then] add white flour as long as you can stir it; beat well; let rise overnight; stir up well overnight; stir up well in the morning; add one cup of chopped or ground peanuts. Pour in a buttered baking pan and set in a warm place to rise; when light bake in a moderate [350 degree] oven for 1 hour.

[1 loaf]

CARVER,
The Peanut

DESSERTS

Desserts mark our holidays and family festivities. What would Thanksgiving be without Sweet Potato Pie or Christmas without Red Velvet Cake? What childhood is complete without learning to bake a cake at your mother's or grandmother's side? Among his many talents, Dr. George Washington Carver was an accomplished cook and confectioner, and a number of his original recipes appear in this chapter. As in earlier chapters, the titles of Dr. Carver's recipes are followed by an asterisk.

"Occasionally one of the houses Dr. Carver visited had two rooms with a dog trot in between, and in such a one he might stop overnight. He would stay with them to Sunday, eat with them . . . as happy as could be over the cakes and blackberry jam prepared especially for him."

HOLT,
George Washington Carver

HALF MOON PIES

CRUST

1 cup sifted all-purpose flour	1 egg yolk
2 tablespoons sugar	3 tablespoons milk,
2 teaspoons baking powder	approximately
¼ teaspoon salt	Fat for deep frying
¼ cup butter	

Sift together flour, sugar, baking powder, and salt into a bowl. Cut in butter. In a separate bowl, mix egg yolk and milk together, then stir into flour mixture. Add only enough of the milk mixture to hold the dough together. Turn out on a floured board, divide dough in half, and roll out each piece to ⅛-inch thickness. Cut into 7-inch-diameter circles.

APPLE FILLING

3 pounds red apples, peeled, cored, and sliced	½ teaspoon ground allspice
⅔ cup sugar	¼ teaspoon ground ginger
2 tablespoons cornstarch	⅛ teaspoon salt
1 teaspoon ground cinnamon	2 tablespoons butter
	⅛ cup apple juice

Toss together apples, sugar, cornstarch, spices, and salt. In a medium saucepan over medium-high heat, melt butter, add apple mixture, and sauté for 5 minutes, stirring often to prevent burning. Add apple juice, reduce heat to low, and simmer 10 minutes. Spoon filling on half of each pastry circle. Fold over the remaining half to form a half moon. Seal edges and prick top with fork tines. Refrigerate until well chilled. In a deep fryer, heat enough shortening to deep-fry the pies to the temperature of 350 degrees F. Fry pies to a delicate golden brown, remove from fryer, and drain on paper towels. Sprinkle the pies with topping below.

PEACH FILLING

½ cup water	1 teaspoon fresh lemon juice
¾ cup sugar	1 teaspoon vanilla extract
4 fresh peaches, peeled, pitted, and cut into ½-inch slices	⅛ teaspoon ground allspice
1 tablespoon butter	½ teaspoon ground cinnamon

In a medium pot, over high heat, bring water and sugar to a boil. Reduce the heat to medium; add sliced peaches, butter, lemon juice, vanilla, and spices. Cook and gently stir an additional 2 to 3 minutes, being careful not to break the peach slices. Drain peaches and spoon onto half of each circle. Fold over, seal, refrigerate, and cook according to directions under Apple Filling above.

TOPPING

1 cup confectioners' sugar or ½ cup granulated sugar combined with 2 tablespoons ground cinnamon

18–20 pastries

Margaret "Maggie" Murray, the third Mrs. Washington
(Library of Congress)

"In the summer of 1892, Margaret Murray became Booker T. Washington's third wife. 'Maggie' was one of ten children, born to a washerwoman by the name of Lucy Murray. She was described as beautiful 'with arched brows, blue eyes, a Grecian nose, . . . and the carriage of a Gibson girl.' (It is said her beauty and carriage inspired Madame C. J. Walker.) Maggie was equally intelligent and ambitious. After receiving her early education from Quakers, she decided to teach, pursuing her degree at Fisk. Approximately one month after Olivia's death, Booker T. was attending graduation ceremonies at Fisk. During his stay, he met Margaret, who had previously inquired about a position with the school. Upon meeting her, Washington was so impressed with her personality, poise, and sharp wit that he hired her to teach English. A year later, she was promoted to the position of Lady-Principal.

"Upon her marriage, she took charge of the women's industries. She also organized mother's meetings and similar work among the plantation tenants. . . . In the upper story of a store on court house square, she and other women faculty members met with the black women of the community on Saturday afternoons, market day. On this day, crowds of country women congregated on the streets to talk, eat peanuts, or dip snuff. . . . 'We tried to teach them self-respect. . . .' They began with the simplest lessons in homemaking."

HARLAN,
Booker T. Washington

APPLE PANDOWDY

3½	cups pared and sliced cooking apples		¼	teaspoon ground nutmeg
1½	tablespoons lemon juice		½	teaspoon ground cinnamon
3	tablespoons maple syrup		1	pinch ground cloves
¾	cup hot water		⅓	cup brown sugar
¼	teaspoon ground allspice		2½	tablespoons butter
				Drop Biscuit Dough

Preheat oven to 425 degrees F. Layer sliced apples on the bottom of a casserole dish. Mix lemon juice, maple syrup, and water together; pour over apples. Mix spices together with sugar and sprinkle over apples. Dot with butter. Cover pan with aluminum foil and bake for 10 minutes. Remove pan from oven and set aside, but do not uncover. Prepare Drop Biscuit Dough. Remove foil from pan and spread biscuit dough over the top of the apples. Return to oven and cook 15 minutes.

DROP BISCUIT DOUGH

1	cup sifted all-purpose flour	2	tablespoons butter
1½	teaspoons baking powder	½	cup light cream
½	teaspoon salt		

Sift together dry ingredients. Cut in butter; add cream and mix quickly. Turn out onto a lightly floured surface and knead for a few seconds.

6 to 8 servings

PEACH PANDOWDY

4½	cups peeled, sliced peaches (about 2¼ pounds)	9	tablespoons melted butter
¼	cup + 3 tablespoons brown sugar	1	cup yellow cornmeal
¼	cup + 3 tablespoons granulated sugar	1½	teaspoons baking soda
		½	teaspoon salt
2	teaspoons fresh lemon juice	1	egg, lightly beaten
¼	teaspoon ground nutmeg	¾	cup light cream
1	teaspoon ground cinnamon	1	teaspoon vanilla extract
¼	teaspoon ground allspice	½	tablespoon peach brandy
		5	tablespoons granulated sugar
		2	tablespoons ground cinnamon

Preheat oven to 350 degrees F. In a medium bowl, combine peaches, ¼ cup of the brown sugar, the ¼ cup plus 3 tablespoons of the granulated sugar, lemon juice, spices, and 3 tablespoons of the melted butter. Arrange peach mixture in a large flameproof ceramic or glass baking dish. In a medium bowl, mix together cornmeal, baking soda, and salt. Add the reserved 3 tablespoons brown sugar. Stir in egg, cream, vanilla, and 3 tablespoons of the melted butter; mix until just combined. Pour the batter over the peach mixture and bake approximately 30 minutes or until the corn bread is cooked through. Combine peach brandy and the remaining 3 tablespoons butter. In a separate bowl, combine the 5 tablespoons granulated sugar and cinnamon to make topping. Remove pandowdy from the oven and turn the oven to broil. Brush the top with the brandy and butter mixture. Sprinkle with topping and broil 5 inches from the heat for 1 or 2 minutes. Serve with French vanilla ice cream.

6 to 8 servings

OLD-FASHIONED PEACH PANDOWDY

4	cups peeled, sliced peaches	1½	teaspoons baking soda
⅓	cup granulated sugar	½	teaspoon salt
2	teaspoons fresh lemon juice	3	tablespoons dark brown sugar
¼	teaspoon ground nutmeg	1	egg, lightly beaten
⅛	teaspoon ground cinnamon	½	cup buttermilk
1	cup yellow cornmeal	2	tablespoons melted butter
2	teaspoons baking powder	4½	teaspoons light brown sugar

Preheat the oven to 350 degrees F. In a medium bowl, combine the peaches, granulated sugar, lemon juice, nutmeg, and cinnamon. Arrange the peaches in a large and shallow flameproof glass baking dish; set aside. In a medium bowl, mix together the cornmeal, baking powder, baking soda, salt, and dark brown sugar. Stir in the egg, buttermilk, and 1 tablespoon of the melted butter; mix until just combined. Pour the batter evenly over the peaches, and bake until the corn bread is cooked through, about 30 minutes. Remove pandowdy from the oven and turn up the heat to broil. Brush the top of the corn bread with the remaining tablespoon melted butter. Sprinkle light brown sugar evenly over the top and broil 5 inches from heat for 1 or 2 minutes, until the sugar melts.

6 to 8 servings

CARROT CAKE

3	cups all-purpose flour	1⅓	cups salad oil
2	cups sugar	2	eggs, beaten
1	teaspoon baking soda	1	cup chopped pecans
1	teaspoon ground cinnamon	1	cup undrained crushed
½	teaspoon salt		pineapple
¼	teaspoon ground nutmeg	1	teaspoon vanilla extract
2	cups coarsely grated carrots	1	teaspoon lemon extract

Preheat oven to 350 degrees F. Combine the first 6 ingredients in a large mixing bowl. Add carrots, oil, and eggs. Beat until well mixed. Add remaining ingredients and stir. Pour batter into two 9 × 5-inch loaf pans or one 10-inch Bundt pan. Bake for approximately 1 hour or until a toothpick inserted in the center comes out clean.

Remove cakes from the oven and allow to cool. When completely cool, top with Cream Cheese Frosting.

CREAM CHEESE FROSTING

4 ounces cream cheese, softened	2 cups confectioners' sugar
¼ cup butter	2 to 3 tablespoons pineapple juice

Cream cheese and butter together. Add confectioners' sugar and blend until smooth. Slowly add pineapple juice until the mixture is just thin enough to drizzle over cake.

10–12 servings

DR. CARVER'S SLICED SWEET POTATO PIE*

Line a deep baking dish with a rich sheet of pastry. Parboil the number of sweet potatoes desired. When two-thirds done, remove the skins, slice lengthwise, very thin. Cover the dish to a depth of 2 inches, sprinkle with ground allspice and a dash of ginger, cloves, and nutmeg. To [make] a pie sufficient for 6 people, scatter around the top in pieces a lump of butter about the size of a hen's egg. Add a teacupful of sugar and 1–2 teacupfuls of molasses. Add 1–2 pints cream, dust a little flour over the top sparingly; cover with hot water, crimp edges, and bake in a moderate oven until done. Serve hot with or without sauce.

CARVER,
Sweet Potatoes

SWEET POTATO PIE

2½ to 3	pounds sweet potatoes		¼	teaspoon ground ginger
3	eggs, lightly beaten		¼	teaspoon ground allspice
1	cup firmly packed dark brown sugar		1	teaspoon vanilla extract
½	teaspoon salt		¾	cup evaporated milk
2	teaspoons ground cinnamon		2	9-inch partially baked pie shells
1	teaspoon gound nutmeg			

Preheat oven to 425 degrees F. In a medium saucepan, boil potatoes in lightly salted water until tender, approximately 15 to 20 minutes. Drain water from pot and shake pot over low heat to dry potatoes. Mash the potatoes and then beat them smooth with an electric beater. Stir in beaten eggs, brown sugar, salt, spices, vanilla, evaporated milk, and sweet potatoes. Pour into pie shells. Bake at 425 degrees F. for 5 minutes, then reduce heat to 325 degrees F. for 40 minutes, until center is almost set but still soft.

Two 9-inch pies

PRALINE PECAN AND SWEET POTATO PIE

If using a traditional pastry pie shell, prick bottom of pie shell and bake in a 350 degree F. oven for 10 minutes until slightly brown. Remove shell from oven and allow to cool.

GRAHAM CRACKER AND PECAN CRUST

1	cup toasted pecans		½	teaspoon ground cinnamon
1	cup graham cracker crumbs		¼	teaspoon ground allspice
¼	cup firmly packed dark brown sugar		5	tablespoons melted unsalted butter

Coarsely grind pecans in a food processor. Add crumbs, sugar, spices, and butter, and blend by pulsing until moist crumbs form. Press crumbs onto bottom and sides of a deep-dish, 9-inch glass pie pan, and set aside.

FILLING

2	eggs, lightly beaten	1	teaspoon ground cinnamon
¼	cup granulated sugar	¼	teaspoon ground allspice
¼	cup brown sugar	1¼	cups heavy cream
¼	teaspoon salt	2	tablespoons butter
⅛	teaspoon ground nutmeg	1½	cups mashed sweet potatoes

Preheat oven to 350 degrees F. Mix eggs, sugars, salt, spices, and cream; add butter and potatoes. Beat well and set aside. Prepare Praline Topping below. Place sweet potato filling in the shell; bake for 30 minutes, then spoon Praline Topping over the filling. Bake approximately 20 additional minutes or until a knife inserted in center comes out clean.

PRALINE TOPPING

2	tablespoons butter	¼	cup cane syrup
¼	cup sugar		Pinch of salt
1	egg	½	tablespoon grated orange peel
1	cup chopped pecans	¼	teaspoon ground cinnamon

In a large bowl, cream together the butter and sugar. Add the egg and beat until the mixture is light and fluffy. Add remaining ingredients and blend well.

One 9-inch pie

"When there were guests, which was often, the children took their meals in the kitchen, after the manner of the Victorian age which held that children were to be seen, briefly, and heard not at all."

HOLT,
George Washington Carver

PECAN PIE

3   eggs
1   teaspoon ground cinnamon
⅛   teaspoon ground nutmeg
¼   teaspoon ground allspice
¾   cup granulated sugar

1   cup dark corn syrup
1½ teaspoons vanilla extract
¼   cup melted butter
1   cup pecans
1   partially baked 9-inch pie shell

Preheat oven to 350 degrees F. Beat eggs, spices, and sugar together. Stir in syrup, vanilla, and butter. Place pecans on the bottom of the pie shell and cover with syrup. (Pecans will rise during baking.) Bake 40 to 45 minutes or until a knife inserted in center comes out clean.

One 9-inch pie

LEMON MERINGUE PIE

PIE SHELL

1¼ cups all-purpose flour
1¼ teaspoons sugar
¾   teaspoon salt
2½ tablespoons chilled, unsalted butter, cut into pieces

¼   cup chilled vegetable shortening
9   tablespoons ice water, approximately

In a medium bowl, sift together flour, sugar, and salt. Cut in butter and shortening until mixture resembles coarse meal. Stir in just enough water for mixture to come together. Form dough into a ball, and flatten it into a thin disk. Wrap in plastic and chill at least 30 minutes. Roll out on a lightly floured board. Start at the center and roll toward the edge, using light strokes. When dough is approximately ⅛ inch thick, press it into a 9-inch pie pan. Bake for 12 to 15 minutes or until golden.

FILLING

1¼ cups sugar	4 large egg yolks
¼ cup cornstarch	½ cup fresh lemon juice
3 tablespoons all-purpose flour	2 tablespoons unsalted butter
¼ teaspoon salt	4½ teaspoons grated lemon peel
1½ cups cold water	

In a heavy, medium saucepan, combine sugar, cornstarch, flour, and salt. Gradually whisk in water. Boil over medium heat for 1 minute while stirring constantly. Remove pan from heat, and set aside. In a separate bowl, whisk egg yolks. Gradually whisk in some of the hot cornstarch mixture. Return warmed yolks to saucepan and boil until very thick, again stirring constantly, about 5 minutes. Remove from heat and whisk in juice, butter, and lemon peel. Cool completely, and then spoon filling into crust, cover, chill, and make meringue.

MERINGUE

3 egg whites	⅟₁₆ teaspoon ground nutmeg
¼ teaspoon cream of tartar	1 teaspoon grated lemon peel
6+ tablespoons sugar	

Preheat oven to 425 degrees F. Beat egg whites until frothy but not stiff; add cream of tartar and continue beating until stiff enough to hold a peak. Gradually beat in sugar; then add remaining ingredients. At this point meringue should be stiff and glossy. Spoon meringue on top of cool pie filling and spread to the outer crust to prevent shrinkage, while mounding high in the middle. Bake 5 to 7 minutes until delicately browned. Cool at room temperature.

One 9-inch pie

"Even when only the family was in attendance, dinner was a formal affair prepared and served by students from the housekeeping department."

HOLT,
George Washington Carver

Serving supper *(Library of Congress)*

"Booker, still in starched collar and tie, would listen as each of his children recited his or her activities for the day. Mr. and Mrs. Washington as they were wont to call each other except when alone, confined their exchanges to generalities. The family might then assemble in the living room where Booker would read aloud from the Bible or Portia would play the piano until bedtime."

STEWART,
Portia

KEY LIME PIE

5   eggs, separated
1   15-ounce can sweetened
        condensed milk
¾   cup fresh lime juice

1   tablespoon grated lime peel
1   9-inch pie shell, prebaked
1   cup heavy cream, whipped

Preheat the oven to 325 degrees F. Beat the egg yolks for 5 minutes or until thick. Slowly add condensed milk, lime juice, and lime peel; then set aside. In another bowl, with clean beaters, beat egg whites until *soft* peaks form. Do not beat whites stiff. Gently fold the condensed milk mixture into the beaten egg whites. Spoon into pie shell. Bake for 20 minutes or until the filling is firm. Serve at room temperature with a dollop of whipped cream.

One 9-inch pie

PEACH PIE

PIE SHELL

1¼   cups all-purpose flour
1¼   teaspoons sugar
½   teaspoon salt
¼   teaspoon ground nutmeg
3   tablespoons chilled unsalted
        butter, cut into pieces

2   tablespoons chilled solid
        vegetable shortening
4   tablespoons ice water,
        approximately

Sift together first 4 ingredients into a medium bowl. Add butter and shortening. Rub with fingertips until mixture resembles coarse meal. Stir in enough water, a tablespoon at a time, until dough begins to come together. Gather dough into a ball; flatten; wrap in plastic and refrigerate at least 30 minutes before rolling. Roll half of dough into a 10-inch circle and fit into a 9-inch pie shell. Roll remaining dough into another 10-inch circle and set aside.

PEACH FILLING

8   ripe peaches, peeled, pitted, and cut into ½-inch slices
1   teaspoon vanilla extract
¼   teaspoon almond extract
⅓   cup granulated sugar
⅓   cup packed brown sugar
¼   cup all-purpose flour
¼   teaspoon salt
2   tablespoons lemon juice
4   tablespoons butter
1   teaspoon ground cinnamon
1½ teaspoons ground nutmeg

Cinnamon sugar (2 tablespoons sugar mixed with 1 teaspoon ground cinnamon)
¼   cup packed brown sugar
2   tablespoons all-purpose flour
3   tablespoons butter
¾   teaspoon ground cinnamon
    Chantilly Cream, page 180
1   teaspoon grated orange peel
¼   tablespoon fresh orange juice
1   tablespoon orange brandy

Preheat oven to 400 degrees F. In a large bowl, combine peaches, extracts, sugars, ¼ cup flour, salt, and lemon juice. Set aside for 10 to 15 minutes. Drain peaches and reserve liquid. Arrange peaches in the pastry-lined pie plate. Dot with butter. Sprinkle filling with cinnamon and nutmeg. Add enough of the reserved liquid to just cover the fruit. Set aside the remaining liquid for later use. Sprinkle cinnamon sugar over second pastry circle and lightly press it into the dough. Cut pastry into 10 strips, ¾ inch wide, and arrange in a lattice pattern over the filling. Trim strips 1 inch beyond rim of pie plate, and fold trimmed edges under lower crust, pinching to seal. In a small bowl, mix the brown sugar with the 2 tablespoons of flour, butter, and cinnamon until crumbly. Without packing, spoon this mixture into the open spaces of the latticework. Place pie on baking sheet and bake for 10 minutes. Reduce heat to 375 degrees F. and bake for 30 to 35 minutes more or until the crust is golden. During baking, baste occasionally with juices that run over and reserved liquid. Cool on rack for 2 hours and serve with Chantilly Cream, to which grated orange peel, orange juice, and brandy have been added.

One 9-inch pie

PEACH SKILLET PIE

CREAM BISCUIT DOUGH

2 cups sifted all-purpose flour
½ teaspoon salt
2 teaspoons baking powder

6 tablespoons butter
2 cups heavy cream

In a medium bowl, sift together the dry ingredients and cut in the butter. Add the cream, working the dough well for several minutes. Cover and set aside.

FILLING

10 to 12 ripe peaches, peeled, pitted, and cut into ½-inch slices
1 teaspoon vanilla extract
¼ cup granulated sugar
½ cup packed light brown sugar
½ teaspoon salt
1½ teaspoons lemon juice
1 teaspoon ground cinnamon

¼ teaspoon ground nutmeg
⅛ teaspoon ground allspice
3 tablespoons butter
Cinnamon sugar mixture (2 tablespoons sugar + 2 teaspoons ground cinnamon)

Preheat oven to 450 degrees F. Combine peaches and next 8 ingredients and set aside. Roll biscuit dough to a thickness of ⅛ inch and place it in a heavy skillet, allowing the dough to hang over the edges. Fill with sliced peaches, dot with butter, and fold the overlapping dough toward the center. Leave the center uncovered and bake for 10 minutes. Reduce oven temperature to 375 degrees F. and bake another 30 minutes or until crust is golden. While pie is hot from the oven, sprinkle it with cinnamon sugar.

One 9- or 10-inch pie

"Julia Ward Howe visited Tuskegee with six feminist companions in the fall of 1898. A moonlit ride from the train station in the balmy air revived their spirits after the

long train ride, and at Washington's home they received a cordial welcome. 'Mr. Booker Washington usher[ed] us into a pleasant sitting room, with such an open fire as one sees only in the land of "far wood." ' "

JULIA WARD HOWE,
quoted in Harlan, *Booker T. Washington*

OLD-FASHIONED BAKED STRAWBERRY PIE

PASTRY

2½	cups all-purpose flour	4	tablespoons chilled solid vegetable shortening
2½	teaspoons sugar		
½	teaspoon salt	4	tablespoons ice water, approximately
6	tablespoons chilled unsalted butter, cut into pieces		

Sift together first 3 ingredients into a medium bowl. Add butter and shortening. Rub with fingertips until mixture resembles coarse meal. Stir in enough water, a tablespoon at a time, for dough to begin to come together. Gather dough into a ball, flatten, wrap in plastic, and refrigerate at least 30 minutes. Roll half of the dough into a 10-inch circle and use to line a 9-inch pie plate. Roll remaining dough into a 10-inch circle and set aside.

FILLING

3	cups fresh strawberries	3	tablespoons butter
1	cup sugar	2	tablespoons granulated sugar
2	tablespoons cornstarch		Whipped cream, for garnish
	Pinch salt		

Preheat oven to 450 degrees F. Wash, sort, and hull the berries. Mix together the 1 cup sugar, cornstarch, and salt; sprinkle over the top of the berries and set aside. Spoon into the pastry plate. Dot with butter. Lightly sprinkle the dough with the 2 tablespoons of granulated sugar, and gently press the sugar into it. Cut pastry into 10 strips, ¾ inch wide, and arrange in a lattice pattern over the filling. Trim strips 1 inch beyond rim of pie plate; fold trimmed edges under baked lower crust, pinching to seal. Bake at 450 degrees F. for 10 minutes. Reduce heat to 350 degrees F. and bake for an additional 30 minutes or until the crust is golden brown. Serve with whipped cream while the pie is still slightly warm.

One 9-inch pie

CHILLED FRESH STRAWBERRY PIE

PIE SHELL

1 cup all-purpose flour	¼ teaspoon lemon juice
¼ teaspoon salt	4 tablespoons ice water
6 tablespoons chilled butter, cut into small pieces	

Preheat oven to 450 degrees F. Mix flour and salt. With fingertips rub butter into flour until it resembles coarse meal. Add the lemon juice and water and work into a dough. Gather dough into a ball, flatten, and dust with flour. Wrap in plastic and refrigerate at least 30 minutes. Lightly knead until smooth. Then roll out to fit a 9-inch pie plate. Prick all over and bake for 15 minutes.

FILLING

Pick over and wash 1 pint of fresh strawberries. Cut in half, if desired, and allow to drain in a paper-lined colander. While strawberries are draining, prepare syrup. Then spoon berries into pie shell.

SYRUP

1 cup crushed fresh strawberries	4½ teaspoons cornstarch
1 cup sugar	⅓ cup unprepared strawberry-flavored gelatin
1 tablespoon fresh lemon juice	

In a medium saucepan, combine first 4 ingredients and cook over medium-high heat until mixture is transparent. Add gelatin, stirring until dissolved. Pour syrup over strawberries in pie shell and chill. Place a dollop of Chantilly Cream on each individual serving just prior to serving.

One 9-inch pie

CHANTILLY CREAM

1 cup chilled whipping cream	¾ teaspoon vanilla extract
1 tablespoon sugar	

Beat cream, sugar, and vanilla until firm peaks form. Cover and chill up to 3 hours before serving. Rewhisk if necessary.

1 cup

APPLE PIE

PASTRY

2½ cups all-purpose flour	¼ cup chilled solid vegetable shortening
2½ teaspoons sugar	
1 teaspoon cinnamon	5 to 6 tablespoons ice water, approximately
1 teaspoon salt	
5 tablespoons chilled unsalted butter, cut into pieces	

Sift together first 4 ingredients into a medium bowl. Add butter and shortening, and rub with fingertips until mixture resembles coarse meal. Stir in enough water, a tablespoon at a time, until dough begins to come together. Gather dough into a ball, divide in half, and flatten each half into a disk. Wrap separately in plastic and refrigerate at least 30 minutes. Roll out 1 piece of dough and line a 9-inch pie plate. Roll out remaining piece into a 10-inch circle; refrigerate both pieces while you make the filling.

FILLING

6   cups Granny Smith apples, cored, peeled, and sliced ⅛ inch thick
½   cup granulated sugar
¼   cup brown sugar
1   teaspoon ground cinnamon
¼   teaspoon ground allspice
⅛   teaspoon ground nutmeg
⅛   teaspoon ground cloves
1   tablespoon all-purpose flour
1   tablespoon fresh lemon juice
3   tablespoons butter, cut into small pieces

Preheat oven to 350 degrees F. In a large bowl, combine apples, sugars, spices, flour, and lemon juice. Mix well and transfer to pie shell. Mound high in the middle of shell because apples will shrink during cooking. Dot with butter. Cover with second pastry circle, and seal and crimp edges. Make several vents in the top crust to allow steam to escape during baking. Bake for 45 minutes or until crust is golden.

One 9-inch pie

"The old stars come up and last forever."

PORTIA WASHINGTON PITTMAN,
quoted in Hill, *Booker T's Child*

"'Go on, Aunt Portia, make a wish! Now cut!'

"Upon the observation of her ninetieth birthday, Portia appeared in a rose-pink suit, . . . graced by a white corsage. Knife in hand, she was poised to cut into a large

Portia Marshall Washington
(Framington College Archives)

chocolate cake, elaborately festooned with confectionery swirls and topped by a mound of butter cream roses as the roomful of assembled guests raised their glasses of pink champagne."

HILL,
Booker T's Child

CHOCOLATE FUDGE CAKE

4	ounces unsweetened chocolate	1	teaspoon baking soda
1	cup packed brown sugar	½	teaspoon salt
3	eggs, separated	¼	cup water
1	cup light cream	1	teaspoon vanilla extract
½	cup butter		Chocolate Filling, below
1	cup granulated sugar		Boiled Brown Sugar Icing,
1¾	cups all-purpose flour		below

Preheat oven to 375 degrees F. In a small saucepan, over low heat, combine chocolate, brown sugar, 1 of the egg yolks, and ½ cup of the cream. Stir frequently until smooth, about 5 to 7 minutes. Cool to lukewarm. In a large mixing bowl, cream butter at medium speed until light and fluffy. Gradually beat in granulated sugar, then beat in remaining 2 egg yolks, one at a time, beating well after each addition. In a smaller bowl, combine flour, baking soda, and salt. Combine remaining ½ cup cream, water, and vanilla. Beat flour mixture into the batter, alternating with cream mixture. Stir in chocolate mixture and set aside. Beat egg whites until stiff but not dry, and fold into batter. Pour batter into 2 greased and floured 9-inch round layer pans. Bake about 25 minutes or until a toothpick inserted in the center comes out clean. Cool cakes in pan 10 minutes before removing cakes from pans to wire rack and cooling completely. While cakes are cooling, prepare Chocolate Filling and Boiled Brown Sugar Icing. Once the cake has completely cooled, spread about 1 cup of the Chocolate Filling between the layers. Spread Boiled Brown Sugar Icing on the sides and top.

CHOCOLATE FILLING

3	ounces unsweetened chocolate	¼	cup butter
1	14-ounce can sweetened condensed milk	1	egg yolk, beaten

Heat chocolate and condensed milk in top of a 2-quart double boiler. Cook over boiling water, until smooth, stirring occasionally. Stir in butter and egg yolk until thick and smooth. Cool to lukewarm.

BOILED BROWN SUGAR ICING

1½	cups packed dark brown sugar	1	tablespoon light corn syrup
⅓	cup water	⅓	cup orange juice
2	egg whites		

Combine sugar, water, egg whites, and corn syrup in top of a 2-quart double boiler over boiling water. Beat at high speed until mixture forms soft peaks, about 7 minutes. Remove from heat; gradually beat in orange juice.

8 to 10 servings

RED VELVET CAKE

½	cup butter		1½	teaspoons baking soda
1½	cups sugar		1	tablespoon vinegar
2	eggs		1	cup buttermilk
1	teaspoon vanilla extract		2	cups sifted cake flour
2½	teaspoons red food coloring		1	teaspoon salt
2	tablespoons cocoa			

Preheat oven to 350 degrees F. Grease and flour two 9-inch layer pans. Cream together butter and sugar. Add eggs, one at a time, beating after each addition. Add remaining ingredients, mixing well. Pour into prepared baking pans and bake 30 to 35 minutes or until cake springs back when lightly touched with finger. Cool in pans on wire rack for 5 minutes. Remove from pans and cool completely.

FROSTING

6	tablespoons all-purpose flour		1	cup granulated sugar
1	cup water		1	teaspoon vanilla extract
1	cup butter			

Mix together flour and water; bring to a boil, reduce heat, and simmer until slightly clear. Cool 2 hours. Cream together butter, sugar, and vanilla. Add the butter mixture to the flour mixture. Beat until light and fluffy. Use to fill and frost cake.

8 to 10 servings

"For her 87th birthday Portia planned a six-day gala. The refreshments included punch; that creamy confection of custard cake, fruit and jam known as Trifle; and German chocolate cake—the recipe given her by her landlady in her own long-ago days as a music student in Berlin."

HILL,
Booker T's Child

GERMAN SWEET CHOCOLATE CAKE

While the following recipe is not that given to Portia in Germany, it is a delicious alternative.

4 ounces German sweet chocolate	2½ cups sifted cake flour
½ cup boiling water	1 teaspoon baking soda
1 cup butter	½ teaspoon salt
2 cups sugar	1 cup buttermilk
4 egg yolks	4 egg whites, stiffly beaten
1 teaspoon vanilla extract	

Preheat the oven to 350 degrees F. Line the bottoms of three 9-inch cake pans with wax paper. Melt chocolate in boiling water and set aside to cool. Cream butter and sugar until fluffy. Add yolks, one at a time, beating well after each addition. Blend in vanilla and chocolate. Sift together flour, soda, and salt. Add flour mixture, alternating with buttermilk, to the chocolate mixture, beating well after each addition until smooth. Fold in beaten egg whites. Pour into pans, and bake for 30 to 35 minutes or until cakes spring back when lightly touched with finger. Cool in pan on wire rack for 5 minutes. Remove from pans; remove and discard paper. Cool completely.

COCONUT-PECAN FROSTING

1 cup evaporated milk	1 teaspoon vanilla extract
1 cup sugar	1⅓ cups flaked coconut
3 egg yolks, lightly beaten	1 cup chopped pecans
½ cup butter	

In a medium saucepan, combine the first 5 ingredients and cook, stirring constantly, over medium heat until thickened, about 12 minutes. Add flaked coconut and chopped pecans. Cool until thick enough to spread, beating occasionally. Use as a filling and to frost only the top, not sides, of cake.

8 to 10 servings

MY GRANDMOTHER'S POUND CAKE

I'm sure you will agree that this is one of the best pound cakes you've ever tasted. It's created with the things you remember best about your grandmother's baking.

1 pound butter, at room temperature	3 teaspoons baking powder
2 cups sugar	1 cup evaporated milk, approximately
6 eggs, at room temperature	2 teaspoons lemon or vanilla extract
3 cups all-purpose flour	

Preheat oven to 350 degrees F. Grease and flour a Bundt pan or two 9 × 5-inch loaf pans. In a large bowl, beat butter until creamy; gradually add sugar and continue to beat until fluffy. Add eggs one at a time, beating after each addition. Sift together flour and baking powder; add to butter and sugar, 1 cup at a time, beating after each addition. Add milk as required, up to 1 cup. Blend in extract. This batter will be thick; it cannot be poured—spoon it into prepared pan and bake 1 hour or until a cake tester comes out clean.

10 servings

"I recall one old coloured woman, who was about seventy years of age, who came to see me when we were raising money to pay for the farm. She hobbled into the room where I was, leaning on a cane. She was clad in rags; but they were clean. She said: 'Mr. Washin'ton, God knows I spent de bes' days of my life in slavery. God knows I's ignorant an' poor; but,' she added, 'I knows what you an' Miss Davidson is tryin' to do. I knows you is tryin' to make better men an' women for the coloured race. I ain't got no money, but I wants you to take dese six eggs, what I's been savin' up, an' I want you to put dese six eggs into de eddication of dese boys an' gals." Since the work at Tuskegee started, it has been my privilege to receive many gifts for the benefit of the Institution, but never any, I think, that touched me so deeply as this one."

WASHINGTON,
Up From Slavery

GIFT CAKE

While it is not known to what use those eggs were put, they were a wonderful gift and inspired this Gift Cake recipe, which calls for 6 eggs.

1¾	cups butter		4¾	cups sifted all-purpose flour
1	cup sugar		½	cup chopped citron
½	teaspoon ground cinnamon		¾	cup chopped pecans
⅛	teaspoon ground allspice		½	cup raisins
6	eggs, separated		1¼	cups chopped candied cherries
2	teaspoons vanilla extract			

Preheat oven to 325 degrees F. Line two 9 × 5-inch loaf pans with brown paper. Grease pans and paper. Cream the butter and sugar until light and fluffy. Add spices and mix well. Add the egg yolks and beat thoroughly. Stir in the vanilla and 4 cups of the flour. Sprinkle the remaining ¾ cup of flour over the citron, pecans, raisins, and cherries, mix, then stir into the batter. Beat the egg whites until stiff and fold in. Pour into prepared pans and bake for 1½ hours.

12 servings

"I rarely do take part in one of these long dinners that I do not wish that I could put myself back in the little cabin where I was a slave boy, and again go through the experience there—one that I shall never forget—of getting molasses to eat once a week from the 'big house.' Our usual diet on the plantation was corn bread and pork, but on Sunday morning my mother was permitted to bring down a little molasses from the 'big house' for her three children, and when it was received how I did wish that every day was Sunday! I would get my tin plate and hold it up for the sweet morsel, but I would always shut my eyes while the molasses was being poured in my plate, with the hope that when I opened them I would be surprised to see how much I had got. When

I opened my eyes I would tip the plate first in one direction and another, so as to make the molasses spread all over it, in the full belief that there would be more of it and that it would last longer if spread out this way. So strong are my childish impressions of those Sunday morning feasts that it would be pretty hard for anyone to convince me that there is not more molasses on a plate when it is spread all over the plate than when it occupies just one corner. . . . My share of the syrup was about two tablespoons, and those two spoonfuls of molasses were much more enjoyable to me than is a fourteen-course dinner after which I am to speak."

WASHINGTON,
Up From Slavery

DR. CARVER'S PEANUT CAKE WITH MOLASSES*

2   cups molasses
1   cup brown sugar
1   cup lard
2   cups hot water
4   cups [all-purpose] flour
1   pint [2 cups] ground peanuts
2   teaspoons cinnamon

½   teaspoon [ground] cloves
¼   teaspoon ground nutmeg
1   heaping teaspoon [baking]
        soda
1   beaten egg
        [Confectioners' sugar]

[Preheat oven to 375 degrees F.] Mix the peanuts, spices, and soda with the flour, which should be measured generously. Mix the molasses, sugar, lard, and water; stir in the flour [mixture], and add the beaten egg last. Bake in a shallow dripping pan and sprinkle with [confectioners'] sugar just before putting in the oven. [Bake for about 30 to 45 minutes, or until cake tests done.]

[12 servings]

"Holidays at the Institute, always very special, were made even more so when one year, just prior to the holidays, Dr. Carver invited James Wilson, his former teacher, now Secretary of Agriculture, to dedicate the new agricultural building.

"When [Dr. Carver] received the [secretary's] formal letter of acceptance and asked little John, son of J. H. Washington and sole office boy, to 'take this to your uncle,' Uncle's face lit up with joy. . . . A tremendous to-do followed, of cleaning, decorating, and erecting arches laden with holly and evergreens and moss, of trimming the Pavillion with native grasses, draping it with bunting and flags. The boys whose duty it was to keep the street lamps trimmed and the chimneys cleaned polished furiously. It was almost Christmas and the fireworks, traditional to the holiday season in the South, were lavishly bought.

"Then [one] evening in mid-December 1897, Mr. Washington and Professor Carver, behind a pair of the principal's swiftest horses, drove to Chehaw to meet the eight-twenty fast train from the East. This was the first time any representative of the federal government [officially recognized] the school, and the white dignitaries were all on hand. About ten the carriages were heard approaching the campus. A boy whipped up the two black horses, and they swung under the triumphal arch—Mr. Washington[,] Professor Carver and Secretary Wilson in a tall silk hat. . . . The band at the entrance under the arch crashed into 'Hail to the Chief,' and one of the professors sent up sky rockets. A thousand boys and girls lined the drive ways, ablaze with dancing lights leaping up into the darkness. It was the time of year when they were bringing in the sugar; the girls waved cane stalks tipped with cotton balls dipped in oil, and the boys flourished pine fagots amid crys [sic] for 'Our Booker.'

"Later, an enthusiastic student would write:

"'Our choir! How it did sing! The ringing notes of the sopranos harmonized most beautifully with the tenor and the bass voices. The visitors were struck to wonderment, and with mouths agape they allowed not one note of the warblers to escape being taken in.'"

HOLT,
George Washington Carver

WHITE FRUIT CAKE

1 pound candied cherries	12 egg whites, stiffly beaten
1 pound candied pineapple	4 cups sifted all-purpose flour
½ pound citron	2 teaspoons baking powder
1 cup white seedless raisins	1½ cups pecans
2 cups brandy	1½ cups walnuts
2 cups almonds	Zest of 1 orange
¼ cup rose water	1 cup light brown sugar
1 pound butter	½ teaspoon ground allspice
1 cup granulated sugar	Brandy
2 teaspoons fresh lemon juice	Grand Marnier
2 teaspoons ground nutmeg	

Prepare fruit by slicing cherries in half, if necessary, and soaking all of the fruit in the brandy for 72 hours. Soak blanched almonds in rose water overnight. Preheat oven to 275 degrees F. Cut brown paper to fit the bottom of a 10-inch aluminum tube pan; grease paper and pan. Cream together butter and granulated sugar. Add lemon juice, nutmeg, and egg whites. Reserve ½ cup of the flour to dust the fruit and nuts. (Dusting prevents the fruit from sticking together.) Sift together flour and baking soda. Thoroughly combine flour and butter mixtures. Dust fruits and nuts and add to the batter. Pour into prepared pan and bake for 3 to 3½ hours. Place a pan of water in the oven to maintain moisture. A fruit cake's flavor is enhanced with age. Age for at least 30 days before serving by storing, well wrapped, in a cool dry place. Once a week or so slightly moisten the surface with equal parts brandy and Grand Marnier.

10 to 12 servings

"The year was 1907 and the chief social event was the marriage of Booker T. Washington's first child, Portia Marshall Washington, to William Sidney Pittman. The whole affair was simple and impressive in its dignity. The electrical division of the school transformed the entire grounds of 'The Oaks' into a blaze of light by utilizing colored lights in the trees, among the rose bushes, hedges, and in the various nooks and corners. Similarly, on the inside of the house, decorations of grasses, ferns, wild Southern smilax,

Wedding entertainment
(Framington College Archives)

white roses with multi-colored lights made the interior most beautiful. [Portia's] father escorted her down the winding stair case as Mendelssohn's wedding march was played. The refreshments were particularly dainty, chicken salad, rolls, cheeses, and olives being served, followed by ice cream in the form of red apples, lilies, white and green colored pears, busts of famous characters, roses and many others of similar kind. The cutting of the bride's cake, a particularly formidablelooking affair, was accompanied with a great deal of merriment. Gifts came from all around the country, including a set of silver from Theodore Roosevelt."

HILL,
Booker T.'s Child

"When I had grown to sufficient size, I was required to go to the 'big house' at mealtimes to fan the flies from the table by means of a large set of paper fans operated by a pulley. Naturally much of the conversation of the white people turned upon the subject of freedom and the war. . . . I remember that at one time I saw my two young mistresses and some lady visitors eating ginger cakes . . . those cakes seemed to me to be absolutely the most tempting and desirable things that I had ever seen; and I then and there resolved that, if I ever got free, the height of my ambition would be reached if I could get to the point where I could secure and eat ginger cakes in the way that I saw those young ladies doing."

WASHINGTON,
Up From Slavery

GINGER CAKES

1	teaspoon baking soda	2½	teaspoons ground ginger
¼	cup warm water	¼	teaspoon ground cinnamon
1	cup sorghum molasses	⅛	teaspoon ground allspice
¾	cup sugar	⅛	teaspoon ground nutmeg
1	teaspoon salt	4	cups cake flour, sifted
	Pinch of pepper		

Preheat oven to 350 degrees F. In a large bowl, dissolve soda into the water, then add remaining ingredients in the order given. Add additional flour if necessary to give the dough the desired consistency for rolling. Divide the dough in half and roll out to a ¼-inch thickness and cut out cakes with a small teacup or glass. Or you can roll them into small round balls about the size of a walnut. Place the cakes on a baking sheet and bake 10 to 15 minutes or until a toothpick comes out clean.

18 servings

GINGERBREAD

1	cup butter, softened	1¾	cups light cream
1	cup sugar	5	cups all-purpose flour, sifted
6	eggs	2	tablespoons ground ginger
1	teaspoon baking soda	1½	teaspoons ground cinnamon
1	tablespoon boiling water	¼	teaspoon ground nutmeg
2	cups New Orleans molasses		Chantilly Cream, page 180

Preheat oven to 350 degrees F. Cream softened butter; then cream together the butter and sugar until light and fluffy. Add the eggs and continue to cream together. Next dissolve the baking soda in the boiling water; mix it into the molasses. Combine the butter and molasses mixtures. Stir in the cream and flour, and then beat until smooth. Add spices, mix well, and pour into two well-greased shallow 9 × 9 × 2-inch baking pans. Bake 40 minutes or until springy to the touch. Serve with Chantilly Cream.

18 to 20 servings

BANANA PUDDING

⅔   cup sugar
½   cup all-purpose flour
½   teaspoon salt
2   cups light cream
3   egg yolks, lightly beaten

2   tablespoons butter
2   tablespoons vanilla extract
1   12-ounce box vanilla wafers
2   cups sliced ripe bananas
    Meringue Topping, below

Preheat oven to 350 degrees F. In the top of a double boiler, combine sugar, flour, and salt over boiling water. Add cream and stir for 10 minutes or until the mixture thickens; remove from heat. Stirring constantly, pour half of the hot cream into the egg yolks. Return egg yolks to the rest of the cream mixture and cook until thickened. Remove from heat; stir in butter and vanilla. Cool slightly. While mixture is cooling, place a layer of vanilla wafers on the bottom of a casserole dish. Alternate wafers with layers of banana slices and cooled pudding mixture, ending with the pudding on top. Make Meringue Topping. Spread over the top and bake 10 to 15 minutes or until golden.

MERINGUE TOPPING

2   egg whites
¼   teaspoon cream of tartar

½   teaspoon vanilla extract
¼   cup confectioners' sugar

Whip egg whites until they hold a peak without being dry; add cream of tartar. By hand, beat in the vanilla extract and sugar.

6 to 8 servings

SWEET POTATO PUDDING

5	cups grated raw sweet potatoes	½	cup unsalted butter, melted
½	cup molasses	½	cup brown sugar
1	teaspoon grated orange peel	½	cup chopped pecans
1	cup light cream	½	cup seedless raisins
¼	teaspoon ground nutmeg	½	teaspoon salt
1	teaspoon ground cinnamon	3	eggs, well beaten
⅛	teaspoon ground cloves		

Preheat oven to 350 degrees F. Combine all ingredients and pour into a buttered 10-cup casserole dish. Bake for 50 to 60 minutes. As crust forms around the edges during cooking, periodically remove the pudding from the oven and stir well to mix the crust throughout. Repeat this procedure several times during cooking. May be served warm or cold. Top with whipped cream or ice cream.

6 to 8 servings

OLD-FASHIONED SWEET POTATO PUDDING

2	cups sugar	⅛	teaspoon ground cinnamon
1½	tablespoons butter, softened	1	teaspoon vanilla extract
1	cup molasses	1	teaspoon grated orange peel
2	cups light cream	3	eggs, well beaten
⅛	teaspoon ground ginger	1½	cups raw grated sweet potato
¼	teaspoon ground nutmeg		

Preheat oven to 300 degrees F. Cream together sugar and butter. Add remaining ingredients, in order, and mix well. Pour mixture into a well-greased 8-cup casserole dish and bake for 30 to 40 minutes or until done, when a wooden pick inserted in the center comes out clean.

8 to 10 servings

OLD-FASHIONED BREAD PUDDING

12	slices stale or lightly toasted bread, diced	1	teaspoon vanilla extract
3	cups light cream	1	teaspoon ground cinnamon
3	egg yolks, well beaten	⅛	teaspoon ground nutmeg
⅓	cup sugar	¼	cup peach preserves
¼	teaspoon salt	½	cup seedless raisins
			Hard Sauce, below

Preheat oven to 350 degrees F. Place bread in a buttered 13 × 9 × 2-inch baking dish. Next blend together cream, egg yolks, sugar, salt, vanilla, cinnamon, and nutmeg. Add preserves and raisins; beat well and pour over the bread. Stir gently with a fork until the ingredients are well blended. Place dish in a pan containing 1 inch of hot water and bake for 45 minutes or until almost set in the center. Serve with Hard Sauce.

8 to 10 servings

HARD SAUCE

1	cup confectioners' sugar	¼	cup cream
4	tablespoons butter	½	teaspoon ground cinnamon
⅛	teaspoon salt	⅛	teaspoon ground allspice
2	tablespoons brandy		

Sift confectioners' sugar into a small bowl. In a medium bowl, beat butter until soft. Gradually add the sugar and beat until well blended and fluffy. Add remaining ingredients and beat until smooth. When sauce is very smooth, refrigerate and chill thoroughly before serving.

[About 1½ cups]

DR. CARVER'S PRALINES*

2	cups brown sugar		2	teaspoons vanilla
½	cup cream			Pinch of salt (1/16 teaspoon)
1½	tablespoons butter		2	tablespoons light corn syrup
[2	cups pecans]			

Cook sugar, cream, salt, and syrup in a saucepan, using a wooden spoon to stir mixture while it cooks. Cook for about 10 minutes until it reaches the soft ball stage. To test, drop a small piece of the mixture in a cup of cold water. If a soft ball forms which can be picked up with the fingers, it is done. Remove from heat, add butter, pecans, and vanilla. Beat until mixture begins to thicken, about 1 minute. Drop by teaspoonfuls on greased wax paper. If mixture becomes too thick, beat in an additional teaspoon of cream.

[Makes a little over 3 cups.]

CARVER,
The Peanut

"*Every girl at the Institute, no matter what trade she was studying, had to learn cooking. During this period Dr. Carver started publishing recipes for cooking peanuts. Taking 14 of these recipes, Professor Carver instructed a class of senior girls. Using the recipes, . . . they served a five course luncheon to Mr. Washington and nine guests— soup, mock chicken [peanuts] creamed as a vegetable, salad, bread, candy, cookies, ice cream, coffee—all from peanuts; and as varied and tasty as one could ask.*"

CARVER,
The Peanut

"Every girl at the Institute . . . had to learn cooking."
(Library of Congress)

CARVER'S CANDIES*

PEANUT BUTTER CANDY

2   cups sugar
2   tablespoons peanut butter

½   cup milk

Blend [all ingredients] together; boil for 5 minutes; remove from the fire and beat steadily until cool. [Break into pieces and store covered.]

PEANUT BALLS

2	cups brown sugar	½	cup boiling water
1	cup [New Orleans] molasses	¼	teaspoon cream of tartar

Boil all [the ingredients] together until the candy will snap when tested in cold water; remove from the fire; add two cups blanched peanuts (coarsely broken); stir until nearly cold; form into balls by rolling between palms of the hands; wrap in paraffin paper to prevent sticking together.

[18 to 24 balls]

CARVER,
The Peanut

PEANUT AND POPCORN BALLS*

½	teaspoon [baking] soda	1	teaspoon vinegar
1	pint [corn] syrup	1	quart freshly roasted peanuts
1	teaspoon hot water	3	quarts freshly popped corn
2	tablespoons butter		

[Mix together syrup, butter, and vinegar.] Cook until the syrup hardens when a little is dropped in cold water, remove to the back of the stove; add the soda, dissolved in a teaspoon of hot water; pour syrup over the corn and nuts, stirring until each kernel is well coated.

[18 to 24 balls]

CARVER,
The Peanut

DR. CARVER'S PEANUT COOKIES #3*

⅓   cup butter
2   eggs, well beaten
½   cup sugar
½   cup flour
½   teaspoon baking powder

½   cup blanched and finely
        chopped peanuts
1   teaspoon lemon juice
¾   cup milk

Cream the butter and add sugar and eggs. Sift the flour and baking powder together. Add the butter and flour mixtures. Then add the milk, nuts, and lemon juice. Mix well and then drop mixture from a spoon to an unbuttered baking sheet. Sprinkle with additional chopped nuts and bake in a "slow oven" [approximately 300 degrees].

[About 2 dozen cookies]

CARVER,
The Peanut

PECAN CRISP COOKIES

1   cup butter
1½   cups dark brown sugar
2   eggs
2¼   cups all-purpose flour
1   teaspoon baking powder
¼   teaspoon salt

½   teaspoon baking soda
2   teaspoons vanilla extract
¼   teaspoon lemon extract
1   teaspoon ground cinnamon
1¼   cups finely chopped pecans

Preheat oven to 350 degrees F. Place butter in a bowl and beat until fluffy. Gradually add brown sugar, beating after each addition, until the mixture is light and fluffy. Add eggs, one at a time, beating well after each addition. Sift together flour, baking powder, salt, and baking soda; add to butter mixture and stir until well blended. Add extracts, cinnamon, and chopped pecans, stirring until blended. Drop by the teaspoonful onto a greased cookie sheet. Space about 2 inches apart and bake for 10 to 12 minutes or until golden.

2 dozen cookies

JUMBLES

½ cup unsalted butter, at room temperature	⅔ cup all-purpose flour
⅓ cup sugar	1 teaspoon ground cinnamon
1 egg	¾ cup raisins
1 teaspoon vanilla extract	¾ cup chopped walnuts

Preheat oven to 350 degrees F. In a large mixing bowl, beat butter until creamy; beat in sugar until well blended. Beat in egg until mixture is light and fluffy, 2 to 3 minutes; add vanilla. In a small bowl, combine flour and cinnamon. Gradually add the flour mixture to the butter mixture and beat until thoroughly blended. Add raisins and walnuts. Drop dough by teaspoonfuls onto a buttered cookie sheet about 2 inches apart. Bake 10 to 12 minutes or until the edges are golden brown. Cool.

2 dozen cookies

BENNE SEED WAFERS

Benne is a West African word for sesame. Frequently used by Africans to thicken and enhance dishes, sesame seeds, brought to the South by African slaves, were thought to bring good luck. Benne seeds were often planted as a border around cotton fields and were used in breads, cakes, and dessert wafers such as these.

1 cup sesame seeds	¼ teaspoon ground cinnamon
4 tablespoons unsalted butter, slightly softened	⅛ teaspoon ground allspice
	⅛ teaspoon baking powder
1 cup light brown sugar	1 teaspoon fresh orange juice
1 egg, lightly beaten	¼ teaspoon grated orange peel
¾ cup all-purpose flour	½ teaspoon vanilla extract
¼ teaspoon salt	

Preheat oven to 325 degrees F. In a heavy medium skillet, toast seeds over moderate heat, stirring until golden brown, about 10 minutes. Immediately transfer the seeds to a plate to cool. Using an electric mixer, cream the butter and brown sugar together. Add the egg, flour, salt, spices, and baking powder, and blend to form a soft dough. Using a spoon, stir in the toasted sesame seeds, orange juice, orange peel, and vanilla until combined. Drop dough by the spoonful onto a well-greased cookie sheet. Bake for about 10 to 15 minutes or until brown at the edges. Allow wafers to cool briefly on the cookie sheet and then transfer to a rack to cool completely.

2 dozen wafers

SUGGESTED HOLIDAY MENUS

FOUNDER'S DAY
Tasty Fried Chicken
Creamy Mashed Potatoes
Creamed Peas and Pearl Onions
Mixed Garden Salad and Garden Fresh Dressing
Sweet Potato Biscuits
Red Velvet Cake
Half Moon Pies

PRESIDENT'S DAY OR
DR. GEORGE WASHINGTON
CARVER'S BIRTHDAY
Sunday Pot Roast
Creamy Mashed Potatoes
Fried Corn
J.R.'s Skillet Corn Bread
George W. Carver Salad
Sliced Tomato and Onion Salad
with Herb Vinaigrette Dressing
Apple Pandowdy
Dr. Carver's Peanut Cookies #3

JUNETEENTH
Roast Suckling Pig
Corn on the Cob
Creamy Potato Salad
Collard Greens With Cornmeal Dumplings
Green Tomato Chow Chow
J.R.'s Skillet Corn Bread

Half Moon Pies
Chilled Fresh Strawberry Pie
with Chantilly Cream
Clove Lemonade

FOUNDING DAY PICNIC
(JULY FOURTH)
Aunt Bay Bay's Barbecue Chicken
Fried Catfish Fillets
Cole Slaw
Festival Salad
Mixed Garden Salad and Garden
Fresh Dressing
Corn Muffins
Hush Puppy Patties
Red Lemonade

FIRST LADIES' DAY TEA
(FEBRUARY 14)
Glazed Country Ham, sliced thin
Peppered Buttermilk Biscuits
Church Social Yeast Biscuits
Benne Seed Wafers
Jumbles
Pecan Crisp Cookies
Dr. Carver's Peanut Cookies #3
Dr. Carver's Pralines
My Grandmother's Pound Cake
Gift Cake

Coffee
Tea
Grandmama's Spice Tea Punch

CHRISTMAS
Roast Turkey and Giblet Gravy
Ham-Flavored Green Beans
Collard Greens With Cornmeal Dumplings
Old-Time Potato Salad
Sweet Potato Casserole
Homemade Cranberry Cups
Church Social Yeast Biscuits
Red Velvet Cake
Pecan Pie
Sweet Potato Pie

NEW YEAR'S EVE
BUFFET PARTY
Glazed Country Ham, sliced
Down-Home Potato Salad for a Crowd
Ham-Flavored Green Beans
Pickled Beets and Onions
Peppered Buttermilk Biscuits
Corn Muffins
Hot Clam Dip
Caviar Dip
Smoked Oyster Log

NEW YEAR'S DAY
Country Fried Chicken
Cousin Margaret's Pigs' Feet
Collard Greens With Cornmeal Dumplings
Black-Eyed Peas à la Carolyn
Orange-Glazed Yams
Corn Sticks
Carrot Cake

HOMECOMING TAILGATE PARTY
Spicy Fried Chicken
Potato and Ham Salad
Sliced Tomato and Onion Salad
with Herb Vinaigrette Dressing
Buttermilk Rolls
Pecan Crisp Cookies
Old-Fashioned Lemonade

ANNIVERSARY DINNER
Garlic Prawns
Quail the Southern Way
Cream of Peanut Soup
Dr. Carver's Croquettes
Ham-Flavored Green Beans
Dr. Carver's Sweet Potato Muffins
Red Velvet Cake
Praline Pecan and Sweet Potato Pie

References

Carver, George W. *How the Farmer Can Save His Sweet Potatoes and Ways of Preparing Them for the Table*, 4th ed., Bulletin no. 38. Tuskegee, Ala.: Tuskegee Institute Press, 1937.

Carver, George W. *How to Grow the Peanut and 101 Ways of Preparing It for the Table*, Bulletin no. 31. Tuskegee, Ala.: Tuskegee Institute Press, 1925.

Carver, George W. *Nature's Garden for Victory and Peace*, Bulletin no. 43. Tuskegee, Ala.: Tuskegee Institute Press, 1942.

"Christmas Days in Old Virginia." *Suburban Life*, December 1907.

Davis, Benjamin O., Jr. *Benjamin O. Davis, Jr.: American*. Washington, D.C.: Smithsonian Institution Press, 1991.

Harlan, Louis R. *Booker T. Washington: The Making of a Black Leader 1856–1901*. New York: Oxford, 1972.

————. *Booker T. Washington: The Wizard of Tuskegee 1901–1915*. New York: Oxford, 1972.

Hill, Roy L. *Booker T's Child*. Newark, N.J.: McDaniel Press, 1963.

Holt, Rackham. *George Washington Carver: An American Biography*, rev. ed. Garden City, N.Y.: Doubleday, 1943.

Library of Congress. *The Booker T. Washington Papers*. Washington, D.C.

Phelps, Joseph A. *Chappie: The Life and Times of Daniel James, Jr.* Novato, Cal.: Presidio Press, 1991.

Stewart, Ruth Ann. *Portia*. Garden City, N.Y.: Doubleday, 1977.

Tuskegee News. Pride Edition, March 8, 1990.

Tuskegee Student Newspaper. October 27, 1906.

Tuskegee University, *The Booker T. Washington Papers*. Tuskegee, Ala.

Washington, Booker T. *Up From Slavery*, 1906. Reprint, New York: University Books, 1993.

Wesley, Phylllis. "Her Activism Was a Gentle Nudging." *Montgomery Advertiser*, March 11, 1990, p.183.

Index of Recipes